Rise and Shine

A Call for Personal Revival

Malcom Ellis

All Scripture quotations are in bold, and are taken from the
King James Version.

Table of Contents

Introduction

Introduction

"...and [Jonah] lay, and was fast asleep. So the shipmaster came to him, and said unto him, 'What meanest thou, O sleeper? Arise, call upon thy God...'" (Jonah 1:5-6)

The question asked is a worthy one: **"What meanest thou, O sleeper?"** What do you mean, professed believer, sleeping at a time like this? Jonah's behavior was totally inappropriate for the situation at hand. This question could have come from the lips of a holy prophet of God, but it came from a heathen who had no personal knowledge of the true God at all. Sometimes the unconverted world seems to have a better grasp of how a Christian ought to behave than many who claim to be born again.

Jonah should have been leading the prayer meeting as the judgment of God came storming in on that ship, but instead he was fast asleep. In his backslidden condition, Jonah had slipped into a spiritual stupor—a Christian coma—resulting in his blatantly inappropriate attitude and actions. This was a moment of crisis, a desperate situation of grave danger, yet Jonah was napping away, snoozing toward imminent destruction, snoring in spiritual obliviousness. Jonah's attitude of rebellion had rendered him so apathetic that he could sleep even through the violent gale of God's chastisement.

Beloved, we are right now in the midst of a tsunami of judgment; a super-cell of hurricane proportions is forming over this nation of Jonah-like believers who are heading in the diametrically opposite direction of the call of God on our lives. The Lord commands us to be holy as He is holy, and we are rushing headlong into the tolerance of greater and greater ungodliness—both in our homes and in our churches. God calls us to be separate and unconformed to the world, yet so many believers seem to have as their ambition a commitment to see how much like the lost world they can be and still consider themselves Christian. And the list of inconsistencies could go on and on.

Because of our fleeing from obedience to the Lord, rather than from sin and idolatry, as we are told to do in Scripture, the storm clouds are gathering and the tempest is upon us. Nationally, culturally, domestically, financially, religiously, emotionally, and spiritually — the winds of judgment are swirling and the ship is rocking, yet many of us who profess to be converted to Christ are sound asleep. Multitudes are indifferent, insensible, and seemingly unaware that anything serious is going on. The fact is that the hour is desperate, but most of us are not. We are drowsy, dozing off, drifting away to dreamland, anesthetized by our own self-deception and false sense of security.

So, I submit to you that the question of the hour is this: **"What meanest thou, O sleeper?"** And the solution to the problem is still, **"Arise, call upon thy God!"** To that end, and with this hope, I offer the chapters that follow, accompanied by the longing that somehow God would stir us up once again to shake off our complacency and repent.

Chapter One

The Problem of Perpetual Backsliding

This particularly troubling turn of phrase ("**perpetual backsliding**") is found in a text from the biblical book of **Jeremiah**. Here it is in its context:

> **Moreover thou shalt say unto them, Thus saith the LORD; Shall they fall, and not arise? Shall he turn away, and not return? Why then is this people of Jerusalem slidden back by a perpetual backsliding? They hold fast deceit, they refuse to return. I hearkened and heard, but they spake not aright: no man repented him of his wickedness, saying, What have I done? Every one turned to his own course, as the horse rusheth into the battle. Yea, the stork in the heaven knoweth her appointed times; and the turtle and the crane and the swallow observe the time of their coming; but My people know not the judgment of the LORD. (Jeremiah 8:4-7)**

It is unfortunate, but true, that the issue of backsliding among God's people continues to be one of the most significant matters at hand. The reason this is so obviously the case is that we are a generation of believers who are desperately in need of revival. Any child of God with the least bit of salvation sense and spiritual sensitivity can see that the great, pressing need of the hour is spiritual awakening on a large scale. And the one and only thing that prevents revival at any given time is the backsliding of the people of God. The unconverted world has nothing to do with biblical revival—it is exclusively the province and responsibility of the born again.

The clearly stated scriptural case is found in these well-known words from **2 Chronicles 7:14**: **"If My people, who are called by My name, shall humble themselves, and pray, and seek My face, and turn from their wicked ways, then will I hear from heaven, and forgive their sin, and heal their land."** The only thing hindering revival from breaking out right now is the backsliding of those of us who are **"called by [His] name."** The very fact that the modern Western Church needs revival so badly testifies that there are some **"wicked ways"** from which we need to turn.

The fact that revival continues to tarry demands that we face the issue of backsliding, including the specific matter of perpetual backsliding. It's one thing to backslide on the Lord, but it's another to remain in that condition long-term. What would cause a Christian to perpetuate a spiritual condition marked by stagnation and fruitlessness instead of quickly humbling himself and repenting his way to revival? Listen to the mercy of God in **Jeremiah 3:22**; **"Return, ye backsliding children, and I will heal your backslidings."** Why would any of us hesitate to answer this gracious invitation to come back to the place of spiritual healing, restoration, and renewed victory in Jesus?

The Lord Himself asked that question in our original text: **"Why then is this people of Jerusalem slidden back by a perpetual backsliding?"** Having raised the question, He then proceeds to give a precise answer. In the surrounding verses, four specific spiritual principles are revealed that combine to address the concern of long-term backsliding.

1. THE PERPETUAL BACKSLIDER DECEIVES HIMSELF ABOUT THE SERIOUSNESS OF HIS OWN SPIRITUAL CONDITION.

The Lord God understands all mysteries of human motivation and behavior. In the case at hand, perpetual backsliding is revealed to be rooted in self-deception.

> Why then is this people of Jerusalem slidden back by a perpetual backsliding? They hold fast deceit, they refuse to return. I hearkened and heard, but they spake not aright: no man repented him of his wickedness, saying, What have I done? Every one turned to his course, as the horse rusheth into the battle.

Right off the bat, the analysis of the backsliders' problem is that **"they hold fast deceit,"** and consequently **"they refuse to return."** Backsliding is perpetuated because children of God self-administer the anesthesia of apathy by means of self-deception. The backslider simply lies to himself about the reality of where he is with the Lord, convincing himself that it's no big deal to not be as on-fire for God as he once was.

This tendency is perfectly illustrated in the Church of Laodicea, as recorded in **Revelation 3:17**: **"Because thou sayest, I am rich, and increased with goods, and have need of nothing; and knowest not that thou art wretched, and miserable, and poor, and blind, and naked."** What a state to be in—pitiful, yet proud; desperately in need of repentance and revival, yet perfectly satisfied and content with the status quo! What hope is there for spiritual renewal when the individual in need of it has so deceived himself that he has no idea of his true condition?

Repentance, which is the key to revival, is impossible until there is an honest awareness that something is terribly wrong. In **2 Timothy 2:25**, "repentance" is identified with **"the acknowledging of the truth."** No one can repent until he is willing to admit the truth to himself. So, backsliding perpetuates as long as believers are deceived about the reality of our heart condition before the Lord.

According to **Jeremiah 8:6**, one of the chief reasons for the flourishing of self-deception among believers is that we can easily get so busy that we never take time to think deeply about the quality of our spiritual lives. The text says, "I hearkened and heard, but they spake not aright: no man repented him of his wickedness, saying, What have I done? Every one turned to his course, as the horse rusheth into battle." What a relevant word to the modern church! Here were people backslidden on God, but totally unaware of the seriousness of the situation because they were rushing around like a horse charging into battle.

It is awfully easy to get so immersed in busy-ness and hurried activity that we never take time to reflect and seek God for help in knowing our own hearts. The plain truth is that "the heart is deceitful above all things, and desperately wicked: who can know it?" (Jeremiah 17:9). Consequently, nothing is more necessary for the believer than regularly allowing the Holy Spirit to search us out and reveal to us our true heart condition. The psalmist prayed, "Search me, O God, and know my heart; try me and know my thoughts: and see if there be any wicked way in me, and lead me in the way everlasting" (Psalm 139:23-24).

If we do not take time on a regular basis to be still before the Lord, to allow Him to show us our hearts, we will unavoidably wind up backslidden. God alone knows the deep workings of our minds and motives, the secret recesses of our drives and desires. We can only know ourselves to the extent that we give Him the opportunity to speak to us and deal with us. It is in this sense that the Lord must "give [us] repentance" (cf. 2 Timothy 2:25), because He alone can enable us to see (and thus acknowledge) "the truth" about ourselves.

A believer perpetuates backsliding primarily because he is deceiving himself about the seriousness of his heart condition. This is usually the result of becoming so enmeshed in the hustle and hurry of life that no time is given to spiritual reflection. The frenzy of daily activity is so distracting that very little time is given to communion with the Lord, such that the searchlight of the Holy Spirit is lost in the shuffle of the momentary and the material.

2. THE PERPETUAL BACKSLIDER DISPLACES SPIRITUAL DEPTH WITH IGNORANCE ABOUT THE WAYS OF GOD.

In **verse 7** the Lord observes, **"Yea, the stork in the heaven knoweth her appointed times; and the turtle and the crane and the swallow observe the time of their coming; but My people know not the judgment of the LORD."** The accusation is that God's people have become more ignorant than the birds of the air when it comes to understanding appropriate behavior. The various fowls know when it's time to come back home, yet God's redeemed children often seem so clueless as to what needs to be done to get right with God.

The statement has been often made, "What you don't know won't hurt you." The truth is it's what we don't know that's killing us in modern religion. Spiritual ignorance results in an appalling shallowness, which is part of the explanation for the perpetuating of a backslidden heart. **Hosea 4:6** contains this essential rebuke: **"My people are destroyed for lack of knowledge: because thou hast rejected knowledge, I will also reject thee..."** Elsewhere in the book of **Jeremiah** the same note is sounded:

> **Therefore I said, Surely these are poor; they are foolish: for they know not the way of the LORD, nor the judgment of their God. (Jeremiah 5:4)**
> **Thine habitation is in the midst of deceit; through deceit they refuse to know Me, saith the LORD. (Jeremiah 9:6)**

One of the chief reasons that backsliders remain in their backsliding is that they are spiritually out of touch and shallow in their understanding of the Word and way of God. So, one of the most important things that any child of God can do is seek to continue to **"grow in grace, and in the knowledge of our Lord and Savior Jesus Christ" (2 Peter 3:18).** To that end, the Apostle Paul recorded his persistent prayer burden for the believers under his charge in **Colossians 1:9-10**: "...we do not cease to pray for you, and to desire that ye might be filled with the knowledge of His will in all wisdom and spiritual understanding; that ye might walk worthy of the Lord unto all pleasing, being fruitful in every good work, and increasing in the knowledge of God."

The fact is that we can only know the living God as He reveals Himself to us. Human beings cannot attain spiritual depth and understanding simply by academic effort. It is the Spirit of God who illuminates the inspired Word of God, enabling the believer to grow and mature and deepen. Apart from an on-going, intimate fellowship with the Spirit, backsliding is inevitable. The Lord alone can open my eyes to spiritual things, making it possible for me to gain new heights and press on the upward way. The psalmist confessed this truth in **Psalm 119:18**; **"Open Thou mine eyes, that I may behold wondrous things out of Thy Law."** No man gets to know the deeper things of God simply by hanging around religion and memorizing Christian clichés. Spiritual depth and maturity are the products of an up-to-date, day-by-day intimacy with the Holy Spirit.

Part of the explanation for the perpetuating of backsliding is that the believer gets locked into an abiding condition of shallow ignorance—what Scripture describes as **"milk"** level Christians (**1 Corinthians 3:1-2**), rather than **"meat"** eaters who are mature enough to feed deeply on the Word of the Lord. **Hebrews 5:11-14** adds commentary to this matter:

> ...ye are dull of hearing. [12] For when for the time ye ought to be teachers, ye have need that one teach you again which be the first principles of the oracles of God; and are become such as have need of milk, and not of strong meat. [13] For every one that useth milk is unskilful in the word of righteousness: for he is a

babe. [14] But strong meat belongeth to them that are of full age, even those who by reason of use have their senses exercised to discern both good and evil.

3. THE PERPETUAL BACKSLIDER DISTORTS SCRIPTURE TO PROVIDE ONLY COMFORT, NEVER CONFRONTATION FOR HIS SIN.

A third piece of the puzzle concerning the problem of perpetual backsliding is found in **verses 8-11** of **Jeremiah 8**:

> **How do ye say, We are wise, and the law of the LORD is with us? Lo, certainly in vain made he it; the pen of the scribes is in vain.** [9] **The wise men are ashamed, they are dismayed and taken: lo, they have rejected the word of the LORD; and what wisdom is in them?** [10] **Therefore will I give their wives unto others, and their fields to them that shall inherit them: for every one from the least even unto the greatest is given to covetousness, from the prophet even unto the priest every one dealeth falsely.** [11] **For they have healed the hurt of the daughter of My people slightly, saying, "Peace, peace;" when there is no peace.**

Backsliding is propped up and promoted by a one-dimensional hearing of the Word of God. It's not that backsliders tune out Scripture all together. It's just that they are only willing to receive those portions of the Bible that soothe them, and they refuse any teaching that makes them uncomfortable or convicted. Like those of the text, they have a selective perception, emphasizing only part of the message of Scripture.

Multitudes of professing Christians would be quick to profess that they believe in the Bible as the Word of God, yet they live daily in direct violation of the teachings of the Word without apparent concern or repentance. How can this be? It must be that they, like Israel of Jeremiah's day, are guilty of tuning out those portions of the Bible that call them to repentance and threaten them with chastisement. Warm applause greets the prophet who says, **"Peace, peace;"** but when the Word from God is, **"'There is no peace'** until you repent and have revival," that is not quite so well received.

Granted, there is much in the Bible that comforts and encourages the believer, even when he is in a backslidden condition. There is always reason to rejoice in the Lord, and the Word of God is full of passages that help and uplift us. Precious promises are seeded throughout the Scriptures—promises that emphasize the faithful love of our Father God, the unconditional grace that is ours in salvation, the rich mercy of the Lord that regards us with kindness and compassion. These things are true and real, and they are cause for great joy.

However, there is more to the Word of God than **"peace, peace."** The Bible also teaches that our Father loves us so much that He cannot and will not allow us to misbehave without consequences. The Scriptures also clearly teach that all of God's children are obligated to surrender fully to His Lordship. Sin is to be regarded as a deadly poison, and from it we are to flee—and if we do not, the chastening rod will be applied in order to save us from ourselves.

Many ministers today, just as most of the prophets in Jeremiah's day, consider it their job to heap loads of encouragement on their listeners. There is no shortage of preachers who feel as if the only appropriate message is, **"Peace, peace."** The message of **Jeremiah 8** is that sometimes that is false prophecy. At times of long-term backsliding, when God is greatly grieved by the spiritual deadness and moral compromise of His people, the appropriate message is a rousing call to brokenness over sin and repentance unto revival. The Lord Jesus said it plainly in **Revelation 3:19; "As many as I love, I rebuke and chasten: be zealous therefore, and repent."** At times the **"rebuke"** of the Lord, with the threat of chastening, is the word of the hour.

14

We dare not focus only on parts of the Word of God, those parts that comfort and soothe, to the exclusion of those truths that confront and call for full surrender. Perpetual backsliding is fueled by a rejection of the whole counsel of God. It is a selective hearing that is willing to receive only those teachings that give us a pat on the back and make no demands on our lives.

4. *THE PERPETUAL BACKSLIDER DENIES THE SHAME AND GODLY SORROW THAT WOULD LEAD HIM TO REPENTANCE.*

Jeremiah 8:12 reads thus: **"Were they ashamed when they had committed abomination? Nay, they were not at all ashamed, neither could they blush: therefore shall they fall among them that fall: in the time of their visitation they shall be cast down, saith the LORD."** This is the result of the preceding verses and principles. Because the backslider is self-deceived, he is spiritually shallow and basically ignorant of the ways of the Lord. That is reinforced by the fact that he is only willing to see part of what the Word teaches. Consequently, he resists any hint that he ought to be ashamed of his condition and that his grieving of the Savior ought to cause him to be broken and contrite before the Lord.

Deliverance from backsliding requires a heart that has become humble before God. There must be a sense of the awfulness of sin that causes the backslider to sorrow and mourn before his Lord. So, where there is no godly sense of shame and sorrow over sin, there will always be a perpetuating of backsliding. The prophet Jeremiah, known as the man who preached through tears, saw this terrible shamelessness take hold of his people as their backsliding was prolonged:

> **...thou hadst a whore's forehead, thou refusest to be ashamed. (Jeremiah 3:3)**

15

> O LORD, are not Thine eyes upon the truth? Thou hast stricken them, but they have not grieved; Thou hast consumed them, but they have refused to receive correction: they have made their faces harder than a rock; they have refused to return. (Jeremiah 5:3)

What causes a member of God's redeemed family to **"refuse to return"** when they have backslidden away from a close walk with Him? It is always the same—they refuse to be broken and contrite over the shameful, subnormal state of their Christianity.

Hear again the familiar words of **Psalm 51:17**: **"The sacrifices of God are a broken spirit: a broken and a contrite heart, O God, Thou wilt not despise."** Less frequently quoted, but equally true, is **Isaiah 57:15**: **"For thus saith the high and lofty One that inhabiteth eternity, whose name is Holy; I dwell in the high and holy place, with him also that is of a contrite and humble spirit, to revive the spirit of the humble, and to revive the heart of the contrite ones."** The one and only hope of real revival, which is the only alternative to perpetual backsliding, is that God's wayward children will begin to be disturbed and upset enough to return to the purity of our First Love.

Brokenness is painful, but the pain is not permanent. It is not the end of revival, but the beginning. Christians are not to live in a constant condition of shame and sorrow, but godly sorrow is the path to renewed anointing and the joy of the Lord!

> Now I rejoice, not that ye were made sorry, but that ye sorrowed to repentance: for ye were made sorry after a godly manner, that ye might receive damage by us in nothing. 10 For godly sorrow worketh repentance to salvation not to be repented of: but the sorrow of the world worketh death. (2 Corinthians 7:9-10)

This is perfectly illustrated in **chapter 8** of the book of **Nehemiah**, where the reading of the Word of God produced great conviction of sin. The people began to weep and mourn, prompting the Lord to send this message; "**...Mourn not, nor weep. ...neither be ye sorry; for the joy of the Lord is your strength**" (**vs. 9-10**). Israel's brokenness was simply the doorway into a fresh experience of the joy of being really right with God.

If revival is to come, if backsliding is to cease perpetuating, then apathy must give way to zeal, ho-hum religion must be replaced with intense passion, and emotional numbness must turn into deep burden and brokenness. I am well aware that this kind of emotional upheaval is not pleasant in the short term. On the contrary, it hurts deeply. It burns like a fire in the heart as the shame of our condition begins to dawn on us. However that burning is not unto destruction, but unto deliverance. The Apostle James wrote of it like this: "**Draw nigh to God, and He will draw nigh to you. Cleanse your hands, ye sinners; and purify your hearts, ye double minded. Be afflicted, and mourn, and weep: let your laughter be turned to mourning, and your joy to heaviness. Humble yourselves in the sight of the Lord, and He shall lift you up**" (James 4:8-10).

These four principles are central in understanding the problem facing much of the church in the western hemisphere today. The marked absence of the person and power of the Lord testifies that much of today's "Christianity" is living in a condition of perpetual backsliding similar to that of the Laodicean Church of **Revelation 3:14-22**. This **Jeremiah** text analyzes the problem, and at the same time provides the remedy for all who are willing to receive it. Based on the truths in the verses under discussion, the cure for backsliding is found in these four things:

- Honesty with God and myself about the seriousness of my subnormal spiritual condition.
- Passionate pursuit of a deeper knowledge of God's ways and Word.
- Willing reception of the whole counsel of God, even when it hurts my pride.
- Humble sorrow and whole-hearted repentance over my foolish and wicked waywardness.

Every one of us who names the name of Christ is living now in one of two conditions—either in revival, or in need of revival. Either I am right with God and my all is on the altar of surrender, or I am backslidden. The single most important question for me to face personally is this: Am I drawing nigh to Christ or drawing back from Him? Or, to use the language of the old hymn, am I "pressing on the upward way," or have I stalled out and drifted backwards?

The Lord has a wonderful life of fullness and abundance available to every one of His children. Backsliding causes us to forfeit the life of blessing, and brings us under the chastening rod of our heavenly Father. Don't live in such a way as to force the Lord to exercise **Jeremiah 8:13** on you: **"I will surely consume them, saith the LORD."** Instead of sitting still and continuing to stagnate in your spirituality, shake off your complacency and repent, and seek God for revival!

Chapter Two

Quenching the Spirit

All sin is against God, even though others may be affected by it. King David, in the process of confessing and repenting of his act of adultery and indirect murder, realized that, although people had been harmed by his sin, the Lord was the true victim—**"Against Thee, Thee only, have I sinned, and done this evil in Thy sight" (Psalm 51:4)**. If that is a true statement—that all sin is against God—then it can be said truthfully that all sin is against the Holy Spirit, because the Holy Spirit is as much God as the Father and the Son. Every sin committed by man is sin against God the Holy Spirit. However, in Scripture there are certain sins that are directly linked to the Spirit, and specific terms are used to speak of them, such as:

- Blaspheming the Spirit (**Matthew 12:31**)
- Grieving the Spirit (**Ephesians 4:30**)
- Doing despite unto the Spirit (**Hebrews 10:29**)
- Resisting the Spirit (**Acts 7:51**)

Obviously, there are certain kinds of sinful attitudes and actions that are specifically offensive to God the Holy Spirit.

The biblical text behind this chapter falls into the category of 'sins against the Spirit of God,' the title coming directly from the Scriptures. **1 Thessalonians 5:19** says, **"Quench not the Spirit,"** and these four words are loaded with significance for any believer who is interested in the subject of revival and spiritual awakening. In reality, the coming of revival really boils down to the matter of finding out where and how the Holy Spirit is being quenched (in our individual lives, and churches), and stopping it!

As anyone can plainly see, "spiritual awakening" is by definition a "spiritual event," meaning that it is the product of the Spirit of God. Genuine revival is not something man can work up in the flesh. It cannot be produced by earthly promotion, advertisement or marketing. Real revival is born of the Spirit; it is a fresh filling and empowering of the Holy Ghost. Revival is an awesome invasion of the manifest presence of God, mediated by the Lord Jesus, and made real by the Holy Spirit in the personal experience of His redeemed people.

How can I hope to have biblical revival (in my life, or church) if the only One able to produce revival is being quenched? To be earnest about the matter of spiritual awakening is to seriously set about repenting of anything and everything that falls into the category of quenching the Spirit. In considering this basic issue, there are three questions that must be addressed.

1. What constitutes quenching the Spirit?

The key to understanding the nature of this sin is found in the word **"quench."** This Greek verb can be rendered, "extinguish, put out, smother, restrain." It communicates the idea of fighting against the influence of a fire, seeking to smother out a flame. It certainly is not out of order to use such a term in relation to the person and work of the Holy Spirit, since one of the primary biblical images of His ministry among us is that of fire. It's not accidental or incidental that on the great Day of Pentecost, when the Spirit was initially given as the fulfillment of the promise of the Father, it appeared as if **"cloven tongues like as of fire"** were resting upon the heads of the disciples (cf. **Acts 2:3**).

We are familiar with the use of the word "fire" to describe the Spirit's operation in the lives of the redeemed. Often revival is spoken of as "the fire of God falling" on His children. It is the particular work of the Holy Spirit to make us "on-fire" for Christ, set ablaze with a passionate love for Jesus. How He longs to ignite in us an inferno of zeal for the glory of God! And our part in the equation is said to be simply to **"quench not the Spirit."** We must not suppress or resist His precious work in us. This is a sister command to the one of **Ephesians 4:30, "And grieve not the Holy Spirit of God, whereby ye are sealed unto the day of redemption."**

The very fact that a Christian _can_ quench the Spirit of God ought to sober us up. Is it really possible for a flesh-and-blood believer like you and me to smother out the fire of the Holy Spirit? Some have a fatalistic view of revival. They feel that God just sends revival if and when He chooses to, and there is really nothing that any believer or church can do about it one way or the other. Too often theologically minded Christians make the sovereignty of God into an enemy of seeking hard after Him for spiritual awakening. I want to state plainly that I believe in the absolute sovereignty of God over all of His creation. But I also believe that the Bible is His inspired Word to the world of men, and that every word in the Word is to be taken seriously. Surely one of the clearest words in Scripture is this plain-spoken command to not quench the Spirit, making it obvious that it is possible for born-again human beings to get in God's way and hinder the Spirit from doing what He wants to do.

It ought to cause us to tremble when we realize that we can each one be guilty of grieving and quenching the Holy Spirit. We, the redeemed of the Lord, can prevent Him from activating revival in our lives and churches! Have you ever noticed the specific wording of **Matthew 23:37-38**, which is the final point in Christ's sermon to the religious leaders of Israel?

> **O Jerusalem...how often would I have gathered thy children together, even as a hen gathereth her chickens under her wings, and ye would not! Behold, your house is left unto you desolate.**

Can you imagine such a thing? Here stands God in the flesh, sovereign Lord of the universe, reflecting back over the years of His dealings with His Old Covenant people, mourning over the fact that repeatedly He **"would"** have revived them, but was prevented by the fact that they **"would not."**

One of the most disturbing things found in the Bible is the lamenting of the Lord. As I've read through Scripture, I've come upon these scattered passages that reflect a God who grieves over His people when they stubbornly refuse to allow Him to move in and through them. One example of this is **Psalm 81:10-16**:

> **I am the LORD thy God, which brought thee out of the land of Egypt: open thy mouth wide, and I will fill it. ¹¹ But My people would not hearken to My voice; and Israel would none of Me. ¹² So I gave them up unto their own hearts' lust: and they walked in their own counsels. ¹³ Oh that My people had hearkened unto Me, and Israel had walked in My ways! ¹⁴ I should soon have subdued their enemies, and turned My hand against their adversaries. ¹⁵ The haters of the LORD should have submitted themselves unto Him: but their time should have endured for ever. ¹⁶ He should have fed them also with the finest of the wheat: and with honey out of the rock should I have satisfied thee.**

The gracious invitation of the Lord is met with indifferent refusal, resulting in their abandonment to their own stubborn choice. But the lament of the Lord is found in **vs. 13**; **"Oh that My people had hearkened unto Me, and Israel had walked in my ways!"**

Here is the solemn reality: it is entirely possible for a child of God to quench the Spirit, and thus prevent the Lord from igniting the fire of revival in his personal life, and even in his church family. Jonathan Goforth, who personally saw the outpouring of revival during his missionary ministry to China at the turn of the twentieth century, made this observation:

> We wish to state most emphatically as our conviction that God's revival may be had when we will and where we will. ...Our reading of the Word makes it inconceivable to us that the Holy Spirit should be willing, even for a day, to delay His work. We may be sure that, where there is a lack of the fullness of God, it is ever due to man's lack of faith and obedience. If God the Holy Spirit is not glorifying Jesus Christ in the world today, as a Pentecost, it is we who are to blame. [1]

What a disturbing thought that you and I can be responsible, and will one day be held accountable, for smothering out the fire of the Holy Spirit—that we can actually restrain the fire of revival and thwart the manifest power of God!

That being said, the big question then becomes, what constitutes the quenching of the Spirit? What does being a spiritual fire extinguisher mean and involve? Answering this question is surprisingly simple: quenching the Holy Spirit is always a matter of disobedience to His leadership.

When the Spirit of God tells me to do something, or cease doing something, and I disobey His leading—that is the quenching of the Spirit. When He speaks to my heart, convicts me of sin, nudges my mind in a certain direction, and I either refuse or ignore Him—that is quenching the Spirit. The essence of this sin is refusing to allow the indwelling Spirit to be in control. Anytime a child of God is conscious of not doing what God wants him to do, he is guilty of quenching the Spirit. The specifics may be as varied as the

---

[1] As quoted by Wesley L. Duewel in *Revival* (Grand Rapids, Michigan: Zondervan Publishing House, 1995), pg. 276.

individuals involved: testifying to an unconverted acquaintance, confessing and forsaking a particular sin, lifting hands of praise in a church service, turning off the TV in order to spend time in prayer, or apologizing to someone who has been offended — to name just a few of the possibilities.

Regardless of the individual details, quenching the Spirit is a matter of disobeying His prompting. When He is trying to do a work in me, and I resist Him; when He is speaking to me, and I ignore Him — herein is the issue of quenching the precious Spirit of God. This is really a matter of domination. If I refuse to allow the Spirit to dominate me, if I attempt to dictate to Him what I will and won't do, if I am less than yielded and surrendered to His control, then I am quenching the Spirit.

There is a wonderful little phrase found in **Acts 15:28** which can easily get lost in the shuffle of the overall context, but I believe it sums up the essence of the God-honoring Christian life: **"it seemed good to the Holy Ghost, and to us..."** That's the whole thing in a nutshell. If it seems good to the Holy Spirit, it ought to seem good to us, and if it seems bad to the Spirit of God, it ought to seem bad to us. There must be no argument between the child of God and the Spirit of God. Anytime there is disharmony between what the Holy Spirit desires and what I want, when my will is in contest and strife with His will, then the result will always be the smothering of the flame of revival. God help us not to snuff out what He is seeking to do in and through each of us!

2. What are the consequences of quenching the Spirit?

The cost of quenching the Spirit is bondage, as taught in reverse in **2 Corinthians 3:17; "Where the Spirit of the Lord is there is liberty."** When the Spirit of God is in control, having His way without hindrance or resistance, the result is a marvelous **"liberty"** in the lives of the redeemed. There will be freedom to read and feed on the Word of God, freedom to preach and be helped by preaching, freedom to pray and believe God for help in time of need, freedom to worship and praise the Lord---to name just a few manifestations of this **"liberty."** Conversely, wherever the Spirit is quenched and grieved there will be a terrific binding, a straight-jacketed kind of religion that is smothering and unsatisfying.

The single most noticeable sign that the Spirit is being quenched is the loss of liberty, or, stated positively, bondage. Instead of freedom, there is restriction. Rather than being loosed in the Lord, we are bound and gagged, hindered from living fruitfully in Christ. My study of Scripture has led me to believe that this essential bondage will manifest in three specific ways.

A. The Bondage of Ignorance.

It is the particular ministry of the Holy Spirit to guide believers into a deepening understanding of spiritual truth. He is our Teacher and Counselor, taking us step-by-step into a fuller comprehension of the Word and ways of our Savior. He is identified as **"the Spirit of truth"** in **John 16:13**, whose ministry is to **"guide [us] into all truth."** Read this wonderful testimony to His work in **1 Corinthians 2:9-12**:

> **But as it is written, Eye hath not seen, nor ear heard, neither have entered into the heart of man, the things which God hath prepared for them that love Him. [10]But God hath revealed them unto us by His Spirit: for the Spirit searcheth all things, yea, the deep things of God. [11] For what man knoweth the things of a man, save the spirit of man which is in him? Even so the things of God knoweth no man, but the Spirit of God. [12] Now we have received, not the spirit of the world,**

but the Spirit which is of God; that we might know the things that are freely given to us of God.

This substantiates the idea, introduced in the previous chapter, that spiritual knowledge and insight into the Word of God cannot be achieved simply by intellectual effort. Only the Holy Spirit can make spiritual things understandable to us. The Apostle Paul prayed for Christians like this: **"That the God of our Lord Jesus Christ, the Father of glory, may give unto you the Spirit of wisdom and revelation in the knowledge of Him: the eyes of your understanding being enlightened; that ye may know..."** (Ephesians 1:17-18). It is simply a fact that God's truth can only be imparted by God's Spirit.

That being the case, what would you expect to be part of the consequence of quenching the Spirit? What kind of toll would it take on a believer who is guilty of resisting the Holy Ghost? It will always result in a remarkable ignorance of the deeper things of God, leading to an astonishing immaturity and shallowness with regard to salvation matters. Two specific passages in the New Testament bear witness to the devastating effects of quenching the Spirit, one of which I quoted in Chapter One (**Hebrews 5:11-14**), and I'll not repeat it here. The other is **1 Corinthians 3:1-3**:

> **And I, brethren, could not speak unto you as unto spiritual, but as unto carnal, even as unto babes in Christ. ²I have fed you with milk, and not with meat: for hitherto ye were not able to bear it, neither yet now are ye able. ³For ye are yet carnal: for whereas there is among you envying, and strife, and divisions, are ye not carnal, and walk as men?**

The sad truth is that many modern believers have been saved long enough to be much further along in their spiritual maturity, and much deeper in the Word of God than they actually are. When the Holy Spirit is not free to have His way in a Christian's life, then neither is that individual going to be free to grow in grace and in the knowledge of the Lord Jesus and eternal concerns. Part of the terrible bondage that results from the quenching of the Spirit is an awful ignorance and abiding shallowness with regard to the things of God.

B. The Bondage of Impotency.

The Holy Spirit is not only the source of insight into the truth, but He is also the one who anoints and empowers the believer for a life of victory in Jesus. Remember the famous words of **Zechariah 4:6**? **"Not by might, nor by power, but by My Spirit, saith the LORD of hosts."** This is how things are to function in the kingdom of Christ. His cause is not fueled by the power of man's fleshly ingenuity or effort, but by the supernatural anointing of the Holy Spirit. The promise of the Father was given by the Savior in **Acts 1:8**: **"Ye shall receive power after that the Holy Ghost is come upon you..."** Again, in **2 Timothy 1:7-8**: **"For God hath not given us the spirit of fear; but of power, and of love, and of a sound mind. Be not thou therefore ashamed of the testimony of our Lord..."** It is the particular work of the Holy Spirit to empower God's people unto a victorious life of obedience to the Lordship of Christ. Given that as true, what would be the consequence of quenching the Spirit? Obviously, if the Holy Spirit is not free to perform His work in the child of God there will be a tremendous deficit in terms of spiritual anointing and enablement. There will be a great bondage of fear and intimidation, and an attitude of spiritual timidity. One of the great and precious promises in Scripture is that of **1 John 4:4**, **"Greater is He that is in you than he that is in the world."** The Holy Spirit, who indwells all born again people everywhere, is the Greater One who is in us. He is able to fill us with the supernatural ability to live fully for the glory of

God. But what if we are guilty of quenching the Spirit? Does it not follow that we would then lose our victory, forfeit the power of God, and end up living in spiritual barrenness and defeat?

When believers smother the Spirit, the power of God is lost to us, and we are forced to try to get by in our own human power. The result of living out of the reservoir of our personal ability is just what Jesus predicted: **"without Me ye can do nothing"** (John 15:5). We end up in miserable failure and religious fatigue. There is a graphic word picture found in the Old Testament which describes in earthy terms the consequence of quenching the Spirit. It is said that, when God's people walk in full surrender to Him, **"Five of you shall chase an hundred, and an hundred of you shall put ten thousand to flight."**[1] What a description of a life of great victory in the Lord! But, the negative is also found there; **"But if ye will not hearken unto Me... ye shall sow your seed in vain, for your enemies shall eat it. ...they that hate you shall reign over you; and ye shall flee when none pursueth you."**[2] What a horrible exchange. Instead of five chasing a hundred and a hundred chasing ten thousand, the Spirit-quenching Christian flees when no one is even pursuing.

In the beloved **John 10:10** passage, the Lord Jesus announced that He has come so that we **"might have life, and that [we] might have it more abundantly."** In **John 7:37-39**, Christ made it clear that it is through the ministry of the Holy Spirit that His abundant life is made personally real to each of His believing people:

> If any man thirst, let him come unto Me, and drink. [38]He that believeth on Me, as the scripture hath said, out of his belly shall flow rivers of living water. [39](But this spake He of the Spirit, which they that believe on

---

[1]Leviticus 26:8

[2] Leviticus 26:14-17

28

Him should receive: for the Holy Ghost was not yet given; because that Jesus was not yet glorified.)

God the Holy Spirit fills us with the abundance of Jesus, empowering us to bear fruit and live in victory to the glory of our Savior. When the Spirit is quenched, we lose the power to live an abundant life, and find ourselves in the bondage of impotency — bogged down in spiritual barrenness and defeat.

C. The Bondage of Irritability.

There is a third aspect to the primary ministry of the Spirit of God in the lives of the born again — He is responsible for reproducing the beautiful life of Christ in those who have been saved by God's amazing grace. That is to say, the Holy Spirit is working to transform us from the world and to conform us to the lovely Lord Jesus. The Bible speaks of it in terms of **"the fruit of the Spirit"** in **Galatians 5:22-26**:

> **But the fruit of the Spirit is love, joy, peace, longsuffering, gentleness, goodness, faith, [23]Meekness, temperance: against such there is no law. [24] And they that are Christ's have crucified the flesh with the affections and lusts. [25] If we live in the Spirit, let us also walk in the Spirit. [26] Let us not be desirous of vain glory, provoking one another, envying one another.**

Real Christian living is not founded on our ability to imitate Christ, but on His willingness to reproduce Himself in each of us, and manifest His life in and through every individual child of God. A large part of the ministry of the Holy Spirit is to communicate the life of the Lord Jesus to us, so saturating our hearts and minds with Christ that **Galatians 2:20** can be our own confession: **"I am crucified with Christ: nevertheless I** live; yet not I, but Christ liveth in me: and the life which I now live in the flesh I live by the faith of the Son of God, who loved me, and gave Himself for me."

There is a wonderful statement concerning the work of the Spirit in the life of a Christian found in **2 Corinthians 3:18; "But we all, with open face beholding as in a glass the glory of the Lord, are changed into the same image from glory to glory, even as by the Spirit of the Lord."** Whenever the Holy Spirit is free to have His way in the Christian's life, He will always be changing us **"from glory to glory,"** from one level of Christ-likeness to the next, moving us further and further toward death to self, so that we may experience and express the resurrection life of Jesus—as in **2 Corinthians 4:10; "Always bearing about in the body the dying of the Lord Jesus, that the life also of Jesus might be made manifest in our body."**

Based on these biblical facts, what would be one of the primary consequences of quenching the Spirit? Beyond question, the fruit of the Spirit would be noticeably missing from the life of one who is guilty of seeking to suppress the Spirit of God. Rather than **"love,"** there will be fault-finding and pettiness. Instead of **"joy,"** there will be constant misery and complaining. In the place of **"peace,"** you would find fret and unrest. And the contrast would go on until each one of the nine-fold components that make up the fruit of the Spirit, which is the life of Christ in a Christian, would be replaced by a nasty, fleshly counterpart.

One of the tell-tale signs that the Spirit is being quenched in a Christian's life is when the beautiful, spiritual fruit of Christ is absent, or at least seldom seen, in the midst of life's frequent frustrations. It is on the heels of the quenching of the Spirit that the category of **"carnal"** is used in the Bible in regard to professing Christians: **"For ye are yet carnal: for whereas there is among you envying, and strife, and divisions, are ye not carnal and walk as men?" (1 Cor. 3:3)**. L.E. Maxwell spoke true with these words: "The church world is full of Christian professors and ministers, Sunday School teachers and workers, evangelists and missionaries, in whom the gifts of the Spirit are very manifest, and who bring blessings to multitudes, but who when known 'close up' are found to be full of self."[1]

A believer cannot quench the Holy Spirit without suffering the bondage of irritability, because the fruit of the Spirit withers away in such a heart environment. The result is always personal frustration and interpersonal friction. Thus the context of the famous **Psalm 51:10-13**: **"Create in me a clean heart, O God; and renew a right spirit within me. [11]Cast me not away from Thy presence; and take not Thy Holy Spirit from me. [12] Restore unto me the joy of Thy salvation; and uphold me with Thy free Spirit. [13] Then will I teach transgressors Thy ways; and sinners shall be converted unto Thee."**

3. *What is the cure for quenching the Spirit?*

The answer to the above question is quite simple—in fact, too simple to be comfortable. The plain truth is that we must repent of all known resistance and receive with child-like faith the fullness of the Holy Spirit. We must confess and forsake all stubbornness, and surrender fully to Him. The biblical cure for quenching and grieving the Spirit is found in **Ephesians 5:18, "Be filled with the Spirit."** The original New Testament Church in Jerusalem is said to have been **"all filled with the Holy Ghost, and they spake the Word of God with boldness" (Acts 4:31)**. To quench the Spirit is to seize control of your life from Him; to be filled with the Spirit is to yield control of your life to Him.

---

[1] L.E. Maxwell, *Born Crucified* (Chicago, IL: Moody Press, 1973), pg. 55.

What must be done to see personal revival and corporate spiritual awakening break out among us? I believe it must involve an individual, settled choice to stop resisting the Spirit, to stop holding Him at arms length as if we do not really trust Him. We must say in essence, "I refuse to be the least bit concerned about what anyone thinks of me but the Lord. I die to my reputation, my convenience, my preferences, and even my religious presuppositions. I want only You, Spirit of God, to be in total control of my life. I surrender myself to do whatever, whenever, wherever You guide, trusting only in Your grace to make it so."

Beloved, we must stop looking for loopholes and escape clauses to avoid doing what we plainly know God is telling us to do. Instead, we must look for every means and opportunity for fuller surrender and death to self. This is how we fan the flame of revival that the Holy Spirit is seeking to kindle. Dr. Bob Jones, Sr. once said, "Sanctification is a supreme desire not to want to have your own way."[1] That's the cure for the quenching of the Spirit—"O Lord, I want nothing but what You want for me! Have Thine own way."

If you find yourself forced to admit that the fire of God is burning low in your life, then help is as close as your willingness to admit that there is a serious problem. Confess that you are in bondage rather than enjoying the liberty of the Lord, and turn your whole self over to Him afresh.

Most of us already know full well what the problem is in our own lives. We've been dealt with by the Holy Spirit in some way that touched us to the quick, and we've tried to defend and justify why we've not surrendered it to the Lord. If we honestly don't know what is keeping the Spirit at bay in our individual lives, then we have ever right to pray with the psalmist, **"Search me, O God, and know my heart: try me,**

---

[1] Bob Jones, Sr., *Bob Jones' Revival Sermons* (Wheaton, IL: Sword of the Lord Publishers, 1948), pg. 68.

and know my thoughts. And see if there be any wicked way in me..." (Psalm 139:23-24). But for most it's not a matter of needing more information; it's a matter of being willing to give in and be changed.

The famous missionary martyr Jim Elliot recorded this prayer in his journal: "God deliver me from the dread asbestos of other things. Saturate me with the oil of the Spirit that I may be aflame. ...Father, take my life, yea, my blood if Thou wilt, and consume it with Thine enveloping fire. I would not save it, for it is not mine to save. Have it, Lord, have it all. ...Make me Thy fuel, Flame of God."[1] Oh, that the God of all grace would give each of us the grace to take such a stand! Dear child of God, hear the Word of the Lord: **"Quench not the Spirit."**

---

[1] Jim Elliot, quoted by Elizabeth Elliot in *Through Gates of Splendor* (New York, NY: Pyramid Publications for the Christian Herald Paperback Library, 1970), pg. 17.

Chapter Three

The Kingdom and the Power

One of the best and most biblical ways to speak of the coming of revival is in terms of the manifestation of the kingdom of God on earth. Christ Jesus taught us to pray, among other things, **"Thy kingdom come. Thy will be done in earth, as it is in Heaven"** (**Matthew 6:10**). There is an ultimate sense in which His kingdom is going to come in full disclosure at the last day. When King Jesus comes to earth again, every knee shall bow to Him, and every tongue shall confess His Lordship, and it can then be truly said, **"The kingdoms of this world are become the kingdoms of our Lord, and of His Christ; and He shall reign forever and ever"** (**Revelation 11:15**). In that sense there is a "not yet" aspect to the kingdom of God as we wait and long for the fulfillment of our Lord's promise to return in glory.

However, there is also a "right now" aspect to the kingdom of God. There is a sense in which the kingdom of God ought to be manifesting in the yielded lives of His people today, as we allow the King to reign unchallenged on the thrones of our individual hearts. The term **"kingdom of God"** has primary reference to His reign and rule. A **"kingdom"** is a realm ruled by a king. Wherever the King legitimately rules, that is said to be his kingdom. So, **"the kingdom of God"** is really His rule in our lives.

To that end, **1 Corinthians 4:20** speaks powerfully: **"For the kingdom of God is not in word, but in power."** Here we have one of the simplest (and most needed) definitions of the essence of Kingdom living found anywhere in the Bible. The Apostle Paul obviously had in mind the "right now" aspect of God's Kingdom, because he wrote of it in the present tense. How does the Kingdom of God work in the here-and-now? What is its real-life manifestation?

The basic message here is that the evidence that any given Christian is truly living under the kingly rule of Jesus is not a matter of saying certain words, but in experiencing God's manifest power. This is a revival text, though the word "revival" is not found in the passage. This divinely inspired sentence stands as an indictment against much of the American church world, and it ought to help cultivate a deep longing for real revival. So much of the religious activity of our day is being done in betrayal of the very essence of the kingdom of God. When there is little-to-no power of God experienced by the church, we know that we have backslidden away from Jesus and have quenched His Holy Spirit. On the other hand, when we are right with God, living under His kingship without rebellion, submissive to His Spirit, the evidence will always be His power operative in our lives and our worship services.

There are two halves to the text verse, and thus two predominant principles with which we must grapple. First, there is a negative statement; then, the positive counterpart.

1. The kingdom of God is not in word.

The order of words in the Greek text is very instructive. It literally reads, "Not in word the kingdom of God, but in power." In Greek sentence construction, words are often placed in a certain order to add emphasis to what is being said. By placing the clause **"not in word"** first in the sentence, the Holy Spirit is using the Apostle Paul to place strong emphasis on this concept. In other words, one thing we must understand is the revelation that God's kingdom is not primarily about verbal statements or intellectual arguments. Kingdom life is not a matter of doctrinal creeds, religious professions, or "Christian" clichés; nor does it consist in high-sounding theological teachings or artistically-crafted sermons.

We need to give a moment of concentrated attention to the specific meaning of the term **"word."** This is the negative principle of the passage, which is given such strong emphasis: **"The kingdom of God is not in word."** **"Word"** (from the Greek *logos*) literally defines as "something said." *Logos* can refer to a single statement, a summary message or teaching, or simply conversational speech. The big point is that the kingdom of God is not defined by verbalizations, no matter how orthodox or impressive the words may sound.

In the surrounding verses, Scripture reveals that Paul was confronting some Corinthian church leaders who were opposing him and his message. **Verses 18-21** read like this:

> **Now some are puffed up, as though I would not come to you. [19] But I will come to you shortly, if the Lord will, and will know, not the speech of them which are puffed up, but the power. [20] For the kingdom of God is not in word, but in power. [21] What will ye? Shall I come unto you with a rod, or in love, and in the spirit of meekness?**

This Corinthian religious crowd was being swayed by some who apparently had "the gift of gab." There was a lot of talk going on, a lot of argumentation and oratory, with no shortage of impressive credentials and religious certifications. But God pierced through the noise and nonsense with this straightforward revelation: **"the kingdom of God is not in word, but in power."**

Do you know how badly this truth is needed in our nation and generation? So many American Christians have come to the place of such comfort-zone religion that we actually think words are enough. If the words being spoken are biblical and orthodox, then that is all that matters to them.

Let me be clear: I believe in the absolute necessity of preaching the Word of God. Clear presentations of the teachings of Scripture are essential to Christianity, and of the utmost importance in growing believers up into spiritual maturity. Anyone who believes the Bible would agree that there is no substitute for sound doctrine, and there can be no real revival apart from strong preaching and surrendered hearing of the Word. Let me quote just a few of the biblical texts that emphasize the centrality of the Word to the experience of God's kingdom:

> **For...it pleased God by the foolishness of preaching to save them that believe. (1 Corinthians 1:21)**

> **How then shall they call on Him in whom they have not believed? And how shall they believe in Him of whom they have not heard? And how shall they hear without a preacher? (Romans 10:14)**

> **Till I come, give attendance to reading, to exhortation, to doctrine. (1 Timothy 4:13)**

> **Preach the word; be instant in season, out of season; reprove, rebuke, exhort with all longsuffering and doctrine. 3 For the time will come when they will not endure sound doctrine; but after their own lusts shall they heap to themselves teachers, having itching ears; 4 And they shall turn away their ears from the truth, and shall be turned unto fables. (2 Timothy 4:2-4)**

Who could deny that courageously speaking (confessing, preaching, and teaching) the Word of the Lord is central to the Christian faith? We ought to be concerned about right doctrine, and we must be continually investing in careful study and clear presentation of the message of the Bible. But we must also remember that **"word"** alone is not enough.

The main point of this precious text is that dry doctrine is not the heart of the kingdom of God, even if said doctrine is soundly orthodox and true to the Bible in every jot and tittle. Anyone can talk a good talk. You can read a reputable book on theology and learn how to say the right words. You can hang around church for a while, listen to sermons and attend seminars, and pick up the lingo of orthodoxy and the spiritual rhetoric of religion. But the question you must face is this: 'Is the power of God operative in _my_ life?' Dr. Lewis Drummond has written on this subject: "The real issue is always, where is the mighty power of the Holy Spirit to convict the lost, sanctify the saints, and bring about holiness of life to the greater glory of God by revealing Jesus Christ."[1]

The personal ministry philosophy of the Apostle Paul can be found in **1 Corinthians 2:1-5**:

> **And I, brethren, when I came to you, came not with excellency of speech or of wisdom, declaring unto you the testimony of God. [2] For I determined not to know any thing among you, save Jesus Christ, and Him crucified. [3] And I was with you in weakness, and in fear, and in much trembling. [4] And my speech and my preaching was not with enticing words of man's wisdom, but in demonstration of the Spirit and of power: [5] That your faith should not stand in the wisdom of men, but in the power of God.**

Too many modern churches have become little more than religious classrooms where congregants are lectured on doctrine and theology. It's not the lecture itself that is the problem, but the fact that the power of God is nowhere to be found.

A tremendous truth is revealed in **2 Corinthians 3:6**: **"the letter kills, but the Spirit gives life."** Now, I say again,

---

[1] Lewis Drummond, *Eight Keys to Biblical Revival* (Minneapolis, MN: Bethany House Publishers, 1994), pg. 159.

we can't get along without **"the letter"** of the Word—we must know what the Bible has to say; we must know the truth and be delivered from the lie. Jesus said, **"Ye shall know the truth, and the truth shall make you free"** (John 8:32). There can be no true freedom apart from the knowledge and confession of the truth of God. But **"the letter"** apart from the manifest work of **"the Spirit"** is only death, which is just another way of saying, **"The kingdom of God is not in word, but in power."** The plain truth is that there is more to Christianity than information, and kingdom living is about something more than just giving mental and verbal assent to a certain set of biblically sound concepts.

Sergeant Joe Friday, of the classic TV series *Dragnet*, had a famous line used in many episodes: "All we want are the facts." But if we have any desire to know God's kingdom rule in personal life and church gatherings, we're going to need more than "the facts," because words alone aren't enough. We must have God's power—which leads us to consider the other half of our text verse.

2. The kingdom of God is in power.

This is the positive counterpart to the negative principle just discussed. We're first told what the kingdom of God *is not*; now we discover what it actually *is*. Recall that the verse literally reads, "Not in word the kingdom of God, but in power." The word **"but"** (in Greek, *alla*) indicates the strongest of contrasts—basically meaning, "But on the contrary." So, the true nature of the kingdom of God is not a matter of talk, but quite the contrary; it's a matter of power.

Our English word **"power"** is a translation of the Greek word *dunamis*, which actually means, "ability, strength, or

---

39

might."[1] In this context, it speaks of the anointing, enabling work of God in the lives of His people. The point is this: the kingdom of God is not about religious fads and fashions, theological statements of faith, or denominational platforms. The kingdom of God comes down to God Himself being powerfully real and active in the midst of the born again, overshadowing our personal lives and corporate gatherings with His glorious fullness.

Remember Paul's greatest burden in ministry, as quoted earlier, was that his preaching be not in human ingenuity, but **"in demonstration of the Spirit and of power."** In that context, the Apostle said that he was **"in fear, and in much trembling"**[2] because of his deep concern that his ministry be not in human ability, but in the manifest power of God. This was no small thing to Paul; he obviously took this issue very seriously, even to the point of fear and trembling. The modern Christian community needs to face this critical question: are we deeply burdened about whether or not the Spirit of God is free to manifest His **"power"** in and through us; or, are we apathetic on that matter, satisfied with **"word"** alone? Carnal contentment with dead, powerless religious activity is the great enemy of the kingdom of God, and thus the greatest hindrance to real revival. It has been my observation, over many years and miles of revival ministry, that multitudes of professing Christians seem to be perfectly willing to live their personal lives and "do church" apart from any sense of the power of God. We have come to define the kingdom of God in terms of intellectual information, but God defines His kingdom in terms of His anointing at work in the lives of believers.

---

[1] Barclay M. Newman, Jr., *A Concise Greek-English Dictionary of the New Testament* (London, England: United Bible Societies, 1971), pg. 49.

[2] 1 Corinthians 2:3

We have heads full of doctrinal facts, but our lives and worship services are alienated from the empowering reality of King Jesus ruling and reigning, and manifesting His glory in our midst. So many have lost any semblance of fire and passion for Christ; they are emotionally detached and numb rather than ablaze with the power of the Spirit. Scripture prophesies of this phenomenon, warning that **"in the last days"** there will be wide scale powerlessness in the ranks of the religious: **"having a form of godliness, but denying the power thereof: from such turn away"** (2 Timothy 3:5).

The Old Testament (**1 Kings 14:25-27**) contains a physical illustration of the spiritual situation facing us today. While Rehoboam was king of Judah, the king of Egypt invaded Jerusalem and, with very little effort, subdued Judah. The Egyptians humbled Rehoboam to the point that they just walked into the house of the Lord, as well as the king's house, and took away everything they saw of value. Here is the key portion of that passage for the subject at hand: **"and [the king of Egypt] took away all the shields of gold which Solomon had made. And king Rehoboam made in their stead brazen shields..."** (vs. 26b-27a). The costly shields of gold had been stolen, and in their absence Rehoboam had bronze shields made to cover up the embarrassment of the situation. From a distance, and to the casual, undiscerning onlooker, bronze shields looked almost like the originals. But a closer examination would always reveal them to be cheap counterfeits.

So much of modern religion seems to be little more than the mass production of bronze shields to replace the precious golden shields bequeathed to us by our King. The mighty presence and power of the Holy Spirit has been forfeited, pushed out by unrepented sin and self-promotion. In His place, in order to cover up for the absence of His power, programmed religion and propaganda abound. We're keeping the plates spinning and the show going on, but where is the glory of God?

When believers are devoid of the power of God—power to be holy, power to be witnesses to Christ, power to produce spiritual fruit, power to be obedient and victorious—then we are denying the very essence of the kingdom of God. Rehearse again with me some of the passages quoted already in earlier chapters:

> But ye shall receive power, after that the Holy Ghost is come upon you: and ye shall be witnesses unto Me both in Jerusalem, and in all Judaea, and in Samaria, and unto the uttermost part of the earth. (Acts 1:8)

> And when they had prayed, the place was shaken where they were assembled together; and they were all filled with the Holy Ghost, and they spake the word of God with boldness. (Acts 4:31)

> For God hath not given us the spirit of fear; but of power, and of love, and of a sound mind. 8 Be not thou therefore ashamed of the testimony of our Lord, nor of me His prisoner: but be thou partaker of the afflictions of the gospel according to the power of God. (2 Timothy 1:7-8)

> Ye are of God, little children, and have overcome them: because greater is He that is in you, than he that is in the world. (1 John 4:4)

We must be bold enough to face such texts squarely, and demand of ourselves, "Are these things true of _me_?" For so many of us, our real-life experience of what we call Christianity has been a matter of struggling through the trials of life and rituals of religion from a sense of duty, rather than experiencing God's power in any significant way. It is imperative that we face the fact that much of modern religion is being performed out of the resource of our own best efforts.

Would it be fair to say that much of American "Christianity" is nothing but lifeless word and powerless activity? And, if that is indeed the case, wouldn't that necessarily mean that we are guilty of violating the very nature of the kingdom of God, and invalidating the essential gospel message that Jesus is alive and well and Lord of all? To say that **"the kingdom of God is in power"** is basically to affirm that wherever God rules as King, His **"power"** will always be manifest in supernatural ways, enabling His people to be and do things they could not accomplish on their own. Again, **Zechariah 4:6** sums up the Lord's kingdom motto: **"not by might, nor by power, but by My Spirit, saith the LORD of hosts."**

What we have on display in much of the modern church world is a manifestation of what men can accomplish for the Lord. Today one can clearly see what *education* can do. There's never been a time when there were more learned and well-studied ministers than now. You can furthermore see what *organization* can accomplish. We have perfected the science of administrating and organizing the faith, and polished programs abound. You can also see what *marketing* can do. There is no shortage of promotional means of advertising the gospel and packaging the message of the church in an attractive way. The only problem is that without the manifest power of God, none of these things have the capability to make a real difference — because true Christianity is not about what we can do for the Lord, but what He can do for us when we surrender our all to His Kingship.

I fear that we have replaced the power and manifest glory of God with church programs and the gimmicks of religion. Where are those believers who would say, "I'm so tired of living life and having church apart from the power of God that I simply _must_ have revival"? Spiritual awakening, which is really just a fresh experience of the kingdom of God, begins with a broken-hearted realization that we're reading things in the Bible that are not real in our lives.

The pathway to revival begins with a desperate hunger for restoration to the place where God's Spirit is free to move in power among us. Oh, that we might come to the point of such spiritual yearning for the Lord that we would no longer be willing to settle for anything less than authentic, anointed, God-empowered Christianity. No substitutes will do, no cheap knock-offs, no bronze shields to try to fool us into the ridiculous notion that we're just fine as we are. The burden of revival is a longing to see God be King over us, so that His manifest presence, which we have sinned away by our apathy and backsliding, can be restored to us. To that end, you find this prayer of the prophet Isaiah:

> **Oh that Thou wouldest rend the heavens, that Thou wouldest come down, that the mountains might flow down at Thy presence, ² As when the melting fire burneth, the fire causeth the waters to boil, to make Thy name known to Thine adversaries, that the nations may tremble at Thy presence! (Isaiah 64:1-2)**

If we have any hope of revival, it will always begin with the willingness to admit to ourselves that something essential is missing from our personal lives, as well as our congregational gatherings. Of course, the condition of the church collectively is simply a reflection of the condition of our individual hearts. We don't just *go* to church, we *are* the church. Whatever we are personally will affect the church collectively. The reason God's power is so markedly missing from our congregational worship services is that His anointing is so alarmingly absent from our personal lives. **Romans 14:17** contains a parallel principle to the one of our original text: **"For the kingdom of God is not meat and drink; but righteousness, and peace, and joy in the Holy Ghost."** The kingdom of God is fundamentally about the Spirit of God having His way in us to such and extent that we are empowered to live right with God, and consequently experience supernatural peace and joy.

We cannot afford to forget that the oft-quoted **Revelation 3:20** was written to a lukewarm church, not the unconverted world: **"Behold, I (Jesus) stand at the door, and knock: if any man hear My voice, and open the door, I will come in to him, and will sup with him, and he with Me."** Christ's invitation to revival begins with a demand that we admit to ourselves that we have pushed Him out of our midst with our lukewarm complacency and our willingness to settle for spiritual mediocrity. We simply must come back to kingdom living, and that means admitting the King back onto the throne of our hearts. He is more than willing to revive us, as we repent of all that has grieved and quenched Him in our lives. His desire is ever toward restoration, and His great delight is in healing and repairing the breach that our sins have caused. His great, merciful heart is revealed in Scripture over and again. Here are two examples:

> **For the eyes of the LORD run to and fro throughout the whole earth, to shew Himself strong in the behalf of them whose heart is perfect toward Him. (2 Chronicles 16:9)**

> **If a son shall ask bread of any of you that is a father, will he give him a stone? Or if he ask a fish, will he for a fish give him a serpent? [12] Or if he shall ask an egg, will he offer him a scorpion? [13] If ye then, being evil, know how to give good gifts unto your children: how much more shall your heavenly Father give the Holy Spirit to them that ask Him? (Luke 11:11-13)**

How He longs to bless us with His kingdom, and anoint us with His Spirit to live out the great and precious promises of His Word! Jesus said (in **Luke 12:31-32**), **"But rather seek ye the kingdom of God; and all these things shall be added unto you. Fear not, little flock; for it is your Father's good pleasure to give you the kingdom."**

45

Nothing would give God greater pleasure than to enable every one of us to experience the fullness of His kingly rule in our lives and our churches. But in order for that to happen, you and I must be willing to face up to the fact that **"the kingdom of God is not in word, but in power."** The modern church culture is (by and large) saying the right words, singing the right songs, making the right confessions — but too often lacking the endorsement of Holy Ghost anointing that validates what we say and sing. At times it is frankly embarrassing to sing, "Power in the Blood" and "Victory in Jesus" when there is no power or victory being manifest in and among us. Not that there's anything wrong with the words we're singing and saying, because they are entirely biblical and true. The problem is that God's kingdom is **"not in word, but in power."**

Spiritually-sounding words can be learned rather cheaply. Read a good book, listen to a good preacher, hang out with born-again people, and you're bound to pick up some kingdom terminology. But kingdom **"power"** can only come by means of the breaking of your pride, the humbling of self before the glory of God, and the abdicating of the throne of your heart before the kingship of Jesus. Before you can honestly say, **"Thy kingdom come,"** you have to be willing to say, "My kingdom go." The simple fact is that God only gives His anointing power to the Christian whose heart is wholly set on Him — sold out to obedience, supremely interested in dying to self and rejecting self-rule, and living exclusively under the authority of Christ Jesus the Lord.

The question must be asked, is our **"word"** being backed up with **"power"**? Is the power of God validating and authenticating what we say and sing, such that our lives and our ministries are identifiable by means of Holy Spirit anointing? It surely must concern any serious Christian when unconverted sinners and backslidden believers can attend our church services, sing our songs, listen to our lessons and sermons, drop money in our offering plates, and walk out the door unmoved and undisturbed about their spiritual condition. Jim Cymbala, pastor of the famous Brooklyn Tabernacle, wrote, "What gains unbelievers' attention and stirs the heart is seeing the gospel expressed in power. …Correct doctrine alone isn't enough. …The gospel must be preached with the involvement of the Holy Spirit sent down from heaven."[1] It is for this reason that the resurrected Christ instructed his disciples, **"Tarry ye…until ye be endued with power from on high" (Luke 24:49)**. We simply cannot get by or get the job done apart from God's enabling power.

We don't need a more clever way of presenting the message. We don't need a more creative sermon series, or more attractive packaging of our programs, or a cuter, more hip way to word what we say. We don't need peppier songs or prettier images to display on our walls. WE NEED THE POWER OF GOD! Otherwise, we are left with nothing but dead religion that cannot change anyone's life. And nothing in the world is as dead as dead religion, because God intends Christianity to be full of life and fire and anointing. So many of our churches are as doctrinally sound as they can be, but the "worship" services are so dull and boring that even genuinely saved people struggle to stay awake and focused, much less those who don't know the Lord at all.

While much of the church is contenting herself with empty, unanointed words, an entire generation is passing out into eternity having never even encountered the true power of the gospel. Multitudes even of the very children of the church, who were raised in Christian homes and attended Sunday School and student ministries all the way to young adulthood, are graduating and going away, never to return to the church. They are seduced by godless educators in the university system, or by the sensuality of secular culture, and

---

[1] Jim Cymbala, *Fresh Wind, Fresh Fire* (Grand Rapids, Michigan: Zondervan Publishing House, 1997), pg. 138.

they're never to be seen again among the ranks of the redeemed. And a large part of the problem is that all they have ever known in church is powerless, unanointed religious talk and activity. When a man, woman, boy, or girl encounters the manifest reality of the Most High God, it makes a difference in them for the rest of their days!

Let's get down to cases. Will you personally say, "Whatever others do, or don't do, I am committed to being discontent until I see the power of God unleashed in my life and church"? God always responds to desperation. When any child of His begins to get desperate for true kingdom life and living, the Lord of glory will manifest Himself to him.

Draw a circle around your individual life, and ask yourself if the kingdom of God is operating in power within that circle. Are you just a bunch of big talk, a religious wind bag who can say all the right words but lack God's holy anointing and power? If so, don't put up with it, not for one more day. This is what revival is all about — returning to the place where King Jesus rules unchallenged in your heart, and thus is free to pour out His blessing, unhindered by any rebellion to His Lordship.

Our heavenly Father is not a miser. He's no skin-flint or tight-wad who hates to bless and empower His children. God loves to show Himself to us, and to lavish on us His empowering presence. His invitation to each one of us is found in **Psalm 81:10: "Open thy mouth wide, and I will fill it."** Press on into the reality of the Lord; never accept a cheap substitute for the real thing. Always remember, **"The kingdom of God is not in word, but in power."**

Chapter Four

The Solution to the Problem

It seems clear enough from the evidence of Scripture that there can be only two basic kinds of Christians: those who are part of the problem, and those who are part of the solution. That may strike you as a bit too blunt, but surely it must be so. When it comes to revival and the restoration of the glory and power of God to His Church, there can be no middle ground of neutrality. Each one of us is either part of the reason that the Lord cannot move in power among us, or we are seeking to let Him have His way with us. Surely we have played religious games long enough, and the time has come for an honest assessment of the situation. We are in serious spiritual need on a large-scale level in American Christianity, and the only hope for us is that we become willing to see ourselves as we really are in terms of our personal contribution to the coming of revival.

The evidence says that we are smothering to death under a blanket of apathy and yawning our way through our religious routines, when we should be panting after God. There is so much spiritual and moral confusion today that even multitudes of people who claim to be believers in Jesus are guilty of embracing things from which we should be fleeing, and we're treating with nonchalance things we should be cherishing. We're upside down and moving in reverse. We're making good time, but we're heading in the wrong direction.

When was the last time you attended a church service where you had any real sense of the majesty and glory of God? Can you remember a time in recent days (even years) when you experienced the living Christ in such a way that you were shaken and changed for having been in that worship

---

service? These things have become foreign to the religious life of many who attend church regularly. We have become strangers to the manifest power of the gospel. The sad fact is that much of our American church life has become an exercise in tedium and boredom. There is very little anointing, living reality, or manifest presence of God. Dull ritual, lifeless religion, powerless teaching, wandering thoughts, drowsy saints, and unimpressed sinners seem to be the realities of the day. One brother has written, "For most…the church has been an experience of grim resignation, of dismay, of guilt, of friction, of conflict, and of perseverance in the rituals."[1]

All of these rather bleak observations are simply other ways of saying that we desperately need a true biblical revival in the church today. And I say again, each of us, as individual Christians, is either part of the problem, or part of the solution. Some years ago I saw this little rhyme on a church marquee:

> What kind of church would my church be
> If every member was just like me?

That is a question worth asking. What kind of influence am I having on my church, my family, my community and nation? How much of a burden for revival would be in my congregation if everyone carried the burden that I have? How much surrender to the Lord and hunger for God's power and glory would there be if all of the church family were identical to me?

In the context of such questions, I would like to offer a text from the Old Testament book of **Habakkuk** that will shed important light on what it really means to be someone used of God to help solve the ills of the religious culture of our day.

---

[1] Robert Thornton Henderson, *Beating the Churchgoing Blahs: An Adventure's Guide to Survival in the Church* (Downers Grove, Illinois: InterVarsity Press, 1986), pg. 10-11.

In **Habakkuk 3:2** we find these words: "O LORD, I have heard Thy speech, and was afraid: O LORD, revive Thy work in the midst of the years, in the midst of the years make known; in wrath remember mercy." Here in plain language we have a revelation of the kind of heart that draws nigh to the Lord, rather than draws back from Him. Here is the testimony of Habakkuk, the prophet of God—a record of his own prayer burden and heart hunger for revival. The little book that bears this prophet's name records the process by which the Lord transformed Habakkuk from the rank-and-file into a spiritual stand-out. Five specific characteristics are given in this one verse that combine to identify what it takes to transfer a believer from the category of "the problem" to that of "the solution."

1. *Sensitivity to the Word of God.*

Habakkuk's prayer begins with the words, **"I have heard Thy speech..."** The Hebrew word translated **"heard"** means "to hear intelligently, to give careful and undivided attention to what is said, to listen attentively."[1] In other words, Habakkuk was paying attention to what God had to say about the situation of his day. Here was a believer with enough discernment to know that the Lord had a word for the hour, and he was listening closely to hear it.

The earlier passages in this precious book indicate that this was not an accidental or haphazard thing in the prophet's life. Habakkuk had made a point of seeking to know the mind of God, so as to understand what was going on in the spiritual realm. **Chapter 2:1** records his intentionality on the matter: **"I will stand upon my watch, and set me upon the tower, and will watch to see what He will say unto me, and what I shall**

---

[1] Spiros Zodhiates, *The Hebrew-Greek Key Study Bible* (Grand Rapids, Michigan: Baker Book House, 1984), pg. 1648.

answer when I am reproved." It reminds me of the repetitive exhortation of the Lord Jesus in **Revelation 2-3; "He that hath an ear, let him hear what the Spirit saith unto the churches."**

The biblical truth is that the Lord is always speaking something to His people. King Zedekiah of Judah once asked the prophet Jeremiah, **"Is there any word from the Lord?"** And Jeremiah answered immediately and without hesitation, **"There is!"**[1] The problem is that there aren't many who have any keen interest in hearing the "now" word of the Lord. The first thing that stands out from our text is that becoming part of the solution to the problem requires a spiritual sensitivity to what God Himself is feeling and speaking over the situation at hand. When the Holy Spirit is being quenched and grieved because of the backsliding of the redeemed, then every sensitive child of God will feel His grief and share it to some extent. There will be a clear and alarming sense that something is dreadfully wrong, and it must be made right.

No one will ever become a prayer warrior for revival, or a catalyst for spiritual awakening, until they are able to sense God's heart and hear His speech. The Lord Jesus, seeking to call His apathetic church at Laodicea to revival, said that in order for things to change they would have to **"hear [His] voice, and open the door"** (**Revelation 3:20**). It was in that very context (**Revelation 3:14-21**) that the great foes of revival are identified as ignorance and indifference:

> **So then because thou art lukewarm, and neither cold nor hot, I will spue thee out of My mouth. [17] Because thou sayest, I am rich, and increased with goods, and have need of nothing; and knowest not that thou art wretched, and miserable, and poor, and blind, and naked.**

---

[1] Jeremiah 37:17

We will continue to be part of the problem as long as we are deceived about our true spiritual condition and unaware of our desperate need for revival. The plain truth is that if we are *unaware* of the problem, then we *are* the problem. The ultimate manifestation of a backslidden heart is always spiritual ignorance and apathy that causes us to be insensitive to how backslidden we are and how grieved God is by our waywardness.

The first issue that must concern the children of God is this: can we hear the Lord's speech? To be more pointed, do you personally know what God is saying to *your* life and church today? Am *I myself* sensitive enough to the Spirit to be aware of how grieved He is at this very hour, and can I hear Him calling the church to repentance and revival? Do we share God's burden for the spiritual situation around us? There are a couple of Old Testament passages that speak directly to this issue from the negative perspective:

> **And in that day did the Lord GOD of hosts call to weeping, and to mourning, and to baldness, and to girding with sackcloth: 13 And behold joy and gladness, slaying oxen, and killing sheep, eating flesh, and drinking wine: let us eat and drink; for to morrow we shall die. 14 And it was revealed in mine ears by the LORD of hosts, Surely this iniquity shall not be purged from you till ye die, saith the Lord GOD of hosts. (Isaiah 22:12-14)**

> **But they refused to hearken, and pulled away the shoulder, and stopped their ears, that they should not hear. 12 Yea, they made their hearts as an adamant stone, lest they should hear the law, and the words which the LORD of hosts hath sent in His Spirit by the former prophets: therefore came a great wrath from the LORD of hosts. 13 Therefore it is come to pass, that as He cried, and they would not hear; so**

they cried, and I would not hear, saith the LORD of hosts: [14] But I scattered them with a whirlwind among all the nations whom they knew not.
(Zechariah 7:11-14a)

Both of the above texts illustrate the seriousness of being unwilling to hear what God is saying to the moment. There are disastrous consequences to spiritual insensitivity, because the only alternative to repenting unto revival is judgment— which leads into the next principle.

2. Fear of the Wrath of God.

Habakkuk's prayer continues, **"I have heard Thy speech, and was afraid."** The man of God, who had taken time and given focused attention to discern what the word of the Lord was for the hour, now admits that he was frightened by what he knew loomed ahead. The Hebrew phrase can be translated, "I am alarmed."[1] The prophet knew enough to be assured that God was not playing religious games with His children, and there was real cause for alarm and concern. Having sensed the depth of the Lord's grief, Habakkuk had become aware that catastrophic consequences were coming.

Being part of the solution to the problem in a backslidden religious culture means that you live in light of the fact that there is a terrible price tag for proud rebellion. If revival does not come, the alternative is not a pleasant prospect for the wayward people of God. In **Revelation 2:4-5** we have a record of a direct threat from the lips of Jesus to one of His own dear churches:

---

[1] C.F. Keil and F. Delitzsch, *Commentary on the Old Testament in Ten Volumes, Volume X: Minor Prophets,* Two Volumes in One (Grand Rapids, Michigan: William B. Eerdmans Publishing Company, 1986), pg. 94 (of Volume Two).

> Nevertheless I have somewhat against thee, because thou hast left thy first love. ⁵ Remember therefore from whence thou art fallen, and repent, and do the first works; or else I will come unto thee quickly, and will remove thy candlestick out of his place, except thou repent.

Have you ever noticed the **"or else"** in that passage? The Lord Jesus threatens His church with a serious penalty if they do not **"repent"** unto revival. In **Hebrews 10:26-31** there is a similar emphasis:

> For if we sin willfully after that we have received the knowledge of the truth, there remaineth no more sacrifice for sins, ²⁷ But a certain fearful looking for of judgment and fiery indignation, which shall devour the adversaries. ²⁸ He that despised Moses' law died without mercy under two or three witnesses: ²⁹ Of how much sorer punishment, suppose ye, shall he be thought worthy, who hath trodden under foot the Son of God, and hath counted the blood of the covenant, wherewith he was sanctified, an unholy thing, and hath done despite unto the Spirit of grace? ³⁰ For we know Him that hath said, Vengeance belongeth unto Me, I will recompense, saith the Lord. And again, The Lord shall judge His people. ³¹ It is a fearful thing to fall into the hands of the living God.

It is obvious that these verses were addressed to believers rather than unbelievers, because it is **"His people"** that God is said to **"judge"** in **verse 30**. Who can ignore the sobering words of **Hebrews 12:28-29**? "Wherefore we receiving a **kingdom which cannot be moved, let us have grace, whereby we may serve God acceptably with reverence and godly fear: for our God is a consuming fire.**"

One of the greatest indicators that we are in serious spiritual trouble is the fact that many professing Christians have so little sense of the fear of God that sin is taken very lightly. They are careless and unconcerned at the very time when they should be greatly alarmed and hasting unto repentance. Throughout both Testaments there is a consistent teaching that there are serious and destructive consequences to backsliding in the lives of God's people. **Psalm 106:29** sums it up: **"Thus they provoked Him to anger with their inventions: and the plague brake in upon them."**

Whenever the professing Christian community is characterized by deadness instead of life, by indifference instead of passionate love for the Lord, and by worldliness instead of holiness, then there is cause for alarm and concern. If you are part of the solution, then you are sensitive to the heart of God to such an extent that you are afraid of the consequences of unrepented carnality.

3. Burden for the Work of God.

Notice that Habakkuk's burden was that God would **"revive Thy work in the midst of the years."** The prophet was yearning to see the Lord make His work "come back to life" right then. The phrase **"in the midst of the years"** means, "right now, at this point in time, immediately."

Hebrew scholars disagree about the exact nature of God's **"work"** for which Habakkuk was praying. Some believe it refers to God's work of judgment that had been revealed in the previous chapters. Others believe it to be God's work in reviving His people so as to render that coming chastisement unnecessary. Whatever the case, the larger principle is that the man of God had a great burden for the Lord to **"revive"** _His_ **"work."** The big point is that it was not Habakkuk's work, or some religious program, or some man-created or flesh-generated activity that formed the prophet's burden. His only concern was that the **"work"** of the Lord would come alive (**"revive"**) in his immediate life and circumstances.

Being part of the solution to what is so glaringly wrong with much of modern Christianity must surely involve this deep heart-hunger to see God's work come alive in the midst of the years. The very word **"revive"** communicates the basic nature of the spiritually-minded believer's burden. It means "to make alive, to restore to life."[1] This verb has the sense of bringing its object back to a state of consciousness and health, and the object here is the **"work"** of the Lord.

Every child of God ought to be deeply burdened over the lack of life in the God-ordained activities of today's church world. Preaching the gospel, teaching the Word, praying, witnessing, reading the Scriptures, and praising God in song—these things ought to be full of life and zeal, but all too often they are not. These holy acts of "worship" are too much of the time characterized by boredom and dull repetition, and sometimes even resentment and hostility. There is too much **"death in the pot."** We are too defeated, too joyless, and too emotionally disconnected. We have turned the dynamic work of God into a boring ritual of dead religion.

To be part of the solution involves a burden that the Lord would reawaken and reanimate His work, that death would be replaced with robust abundant life, that dullness and boredom would give way to the exhilarating reality of an encounter with the living God. Brian Edwards wrote this:

> One of the marks of a true awakening by the Holy Spirit [is] when things once considered dull and tedious become alive and meaningful in such a way that they cannot be left alone. Prayer, preaching and

---

[1] Spiros Zodhiates, *The Hebrew-Greek Key Study Bible* (Grand Rapids, Michigan: Baker Book House, 1984), pg. 1591.

worship become the most enjoyable activities in life for both young people and old.[1]

4. Hunger for the Witness of God.

Notice the particular wording of this phrase in Habakkuk's prayer: **"in the midst of the years make known."** This raises the question, "Make *what* known?" The answer must be that Habakkuk's real heart-desire was that the Lord would make Himself known, so that men might see God for who He really is. Andrew Murray wrote, "God can bestow no higher favor than to make Himself known."[2] Some translations insert the pronoun "it" into the verse, meaning, "Make Your work known." Either way, the deepest longing in this prophet's soul was for the Lord God to show Himself strong in the midst of His people in an empowering and enlivening way.

This seems to be exactly the same heart-cry as that of the prophet Isaiah in **Isaiah 64:1-2**, which has been quoted in earlier chapters. Here it is again:

> **Oh that Thou wouldest rend the heavens, that Thou wouldest come down, that the mountains might flow down at Thy presence, [2] ...to make Thy name known to Thine adversaries, that the nations may tremble at Thy presence!**

The essence of the prophet's concern is that the Lord would make Himself known. **Psalm 74:22** reflects the same desire: **"Arise, O God, plead Thine own cause: remember how the foolish man reproacheth Thee daily."**

[1] Brian H. Edwards, *Revival! A People Saturated with God* (Darlington, Co. Durham, England: Evangelical Press, 1990), pg. 146.

[2] Andrew Murray, *Revival* (Minneapolis, Minn.: Bethany House Publishers, 1990), pg. 53.

Every Christian who is part of the solution to the spiritual crisis in contemporary church life shares this desire: that God would manifest His power and glory in the here-and now. All of us who know Christ ought to be consumed with a burning desire to see our Lord worshipped and reverenced as He deserves. It should concern us to the point of fasting and prayer, even to the point of crying out to God to reveal Himself among His children, so that the unconverted community and the flippant, fleshly church would be shaken by the majesty of the High King of Heaven.

Many in the church know the Lord only as the God of the past; they know of the Bible stories and personal testimonies of what He has done in years gone by. Many know Him as the God of the future; they expect His glorious second coming and final triumph. But we need to know Him as the God of today; a God who can and will manifest Himself in the right now in revival power. That's what the cry, **"in the midst of the years make known,"** is all about.

Becoming part of the solution requires a burning desire to see God manifest Himself in a powerful, glorious way. The deep yearning of **Psalm 42:1-3** expresses it so well:

> **As the hart panteth after the water brooks, so panteth my soul after Thee, O God. 2 My soul thirsteth for God, for the living God: when shall I come and appear before God? 3 My tears have been my meat day and night, while they continually say unto me, Where is thy God?**

May God raise up a remnant among us who will be driven by an aching desire for the Lord to make Himself and His glorious reality known in a manifest way. Oh, that He would break through the cold, formal religion that so prevails today with a volcanic eruption of His power and glory!

5. Hope in the Willingness of God.

The prophet cried out, **"In the midst of wrath remember mercy."** Habakkuk knew that he had only one basis for praying as he was, and that was the mercy of God. Of all the things said of the Lord, none is more precious than the revelation that He is **"rich in mercy" (Ephesians 2:4)**.

It seems clear that becoming part of the solution involves a firm faith that God is merciful, and that it delights Him most of all to revive His work and heal the backslidings of His people. Our God takes no pleasure in wrath and judgment.

> **Therefore, O thou son of man, speak unto the house of Israel; Thus ye speak, saying, If our transgressions and our sins be upon us, and we pine away in them, how should we then live? [11] Say unto them, As I live, saith the Lord GOD, I have no pleasure in the death of the wicked; but that the wicked turn from his way and live: turn ye, turn ye from your evil ways; for why will ye die, O house of Israel? (Ezekiel 33:10-11)**

This is reiterated in **Lamentations 3:31-33**:

> **For the Lord will not cast off for ever: [32] But though He cause grief, yet will He have compassion according to the multitude of His mercies. [33] For He doth not afflict willingly nor grieve the children of men.**

The Lord has over-and-again revealed Himself as a God who loves to restore the wayward and revive the backslidden. For instance, **Jeremiah 3:12; "Return, thou backsliding Israel, saith the LORD, and I will not cause Mine anger to fall upon you: for I am merciful, saith the LORD..."** In the New Testament story of the prodigal son (**Luke 15:11-24**), the errant child, having reached a place of repentance, came back to his father still stinking from the hog pen of his foolishness. But the boy, who had been such a heartache and embarrassment to his dad, found himself being greeted not with a clinched fist and cold stare, but with kisses and hugs and celebration that he had come home at last.

Being part of the solution involves the realization that God Himself longs to show mercy and give revival to His children. That doesn't mean that He will turn a blind eye to our backsliding, because to do so would be lazy irresponsibility rather than true love and mercy. No parent can be said to love his children if he isn't willing to do the hard work of correcting them when they do wrong and training them to do right. The Heavenly Father loves us too much to let us get away with carnality. Christ Himself said, **"As many as I love I rebuke and chasten: be zealous therefore, and repent."**[1] But, even in the midst of severe chastening, we can confidently know that the purpose of it all is to move us into repentance so that we can be revived and enjoy the abundant life that Jesus purchased for us on the bloody cross.

> **This I recall to my mind, therefore have I hope. 22 It is of the LORD'S mercies that we are not consumed, because His compassions fail not. 23 They are new every morning: great is Thy faithfulness. 24 The LORD is my portion, saith my soul; therefore will I hope in Him. (Lamentations 3:21-24)**

We need never hesitate to appeal to the mercy of the Lord because there is nothing He loves better than to show kindness to repentant sinners and to give grace to those who will humble themselves and admit their great need of rescue.

---

[1] Revelation 3:19

These are the things that combine to transform a believer into a prayer warrior for revival. These five principles are absolutely necessary if you are interested in ensuring that you are a spiritual plus rather than a minus. The personal question then becomes, "Is any of this in _me_?" Can I recognize any similarity between my spirituality and that of Habakkuk? Does my own heart resonate with this biblical text? Am I a part of what is destroying Christianity in this generation, or am I part of that which will remedy the situation?

A prayer of Habakkuk the prophet...
"O LORD, I have heard Thy speech, and was afraid:
O LORD, revive Thy work in the midst of the years,
In the midst of the years make known;
In wrath remember mercy."

Chapter Five

An Appetite for God

In the decades that I have spent preaching Bible Conferences and local church revival meetings, I have observed this increasing trend in modern religious life: we are a people who are easily distracted from eternal concerns and who have very little time or interest for serious seeking after the Lord. Most of us would readily admit that the greatest needs we have in our personal Christianity are more consistency in prayer and devotional feeding on the Word. It's not that we don't know what we ought to be doing; it's just that we keep supplanting spiritual things with the momentary distractions of life and living.

Our prayerlessness, our non-existent private worship, and our haphazard handling of the Bible all testify against us that something is terribly wrong in our priorities. If the problem is not lack of information, then wherein is the difficulty? We are so prone to focus on symptoms that sometimes we neglect to go to the root of the matter. What's causing me to be so willing to neglect the prayer closet? What's behind my tendency to go for days and weeks without any quality time alone with my Savior in communion around His inspired Word? The root of the issue can only be that I have no real appetite for God.

I have come to believe this basic principle: pouring out my heart in prayer and filling up my mind with the Word are the natural expressions of a heart that is desperately hungry for the Lord. The only reasonable explanation for our neglect of these spiritual disciplines is that we just don't want Jesus badly enough. In the spiritual classic, *The Practice of the*

Presence of God, these sentiments were observed in the man of God called Brother Lawrence: "He complains much of our blindness, and cries often that we are to be pitied who content ourselves with so little."[1] We are too easily satisfied with less than the fullness of the Lord, which is why everything in the world seems to take precedence over our devotional lives. We just don't really want God—at least not compared to how much we want other things. Don't you believe that we will always seek to satisfy our deepest and most clamorous appetites, whatever they are?

If I have a recurring problem with debilitating headaches, I want something to give me relief. So, I go to a physician and ask for a painkiller to deal with my symptoms. But if the doctor is worth his salt, he will do more than scribble down a prescription. He'll examine me to find out why this problem persists; he'll run some tests and do some probing into the situation. And if he finds a tumor pressing on my brain, he doesn't just give me a bottle of medicine to cover up the pain; he suggests a treatment to deal with the root issue.

We've just got to go deeper than symptoms. We must be willing to do the painful work of cutting down to the reason for our persistent spiritual problems. And that must be a lack of heart-hunger for the Lord. When we have an appetite for Him, then prayer and time in the Word are not irksome duties to be performed in order to earn our religious merit badge; they become the joy and rejoicing of our hearts. Richard Foster put it like this: "Have a kind of dissatisfied satisfaction—glad for all the good God has given you and yet longing for more. More love. More power. More grace. More gifting."[2] It is our hunger and thirst for deeper intimacy and

---

[1] Brother Lawrence, *The Practice of the Presence of God* (White Plains, NY: Peter Pauper Press, Inc., 1963), pg. 39.

[2] Richard J. Foster, *Streams of Living Water: Celebrating the Great Traditions of Christian Faith* (New York: HarperCollins, 1998), pg. 132.

fuller knowledge of our Savior that keeps us in hot pursuit of spiritual things. When we have those kinds of spiritual longings, we don't have to "make time" to pray and feast on the Word. We find ourselves drawn irresistibly to the place of private devotion and worship, and it becomes the sweetest bread out of Heaven's oven to spend time seeking the face of our God.

The Scriptures speak often of the importance of "hungering and thirsting" after the Lord. I will use **Psalm 63:1-8** as the focus of this chapter because it so perfectly represents the great principles surrounding this theme:

> **O God, thou art my God; early will I seek Thee: my soul thirsteth for Thee, my flesh longeth for Thee in a dry and thirsty land, where no water is; ² To see Thy power and Thy glory, so as I have seen Thee in the sanctuary. ³ Because Thy lovingkindness is better than life, my lips shall praise Thee. ⁴ Thus will I bless Thee while I live: I will lift up my hands in Thy name. ⁵ My soul shall be satisfied as with marrow and fatness; and my mouth shall praise Thee with joyful lips: ⁶ When I remember Thee upon my bed, and meditate on Thee in the night watches. ⁷ Because Thou hast been my help, therefore in the shadow of Thy wings will I rejoice. ⁸ My soul followeth hard after Thee: Thy right hand upholdeth me.**

The cultivation of this kind of appetite for God is the one thing needful in our quest to have personal revival and to be a catalyst for church-wide spiritual awakening. We've got to personally give ourselves to becoming the kind of Christian who is obsessed with this magnificent desire: "I must know God better! He must increase, and I must decrease! I must be filled more and more with Himself!" This kind of desperation for the Lord will fix everything that is out of order in our lives and churches. To help toward that end, notice four principles from **Psalm 63**.

1. The Eagerness of Spiritual Appetite.

The wording of **verse 1** captures the intensity of the psalmist's desire: **"O God, Thou art my God; early will I seek Thee: my soul thirsteth for Thee, my flesh longeth for Thee in a dry and thirsty land, where no water is."** The phrasing of the sentence communicates an eager longing for the Lord that affected the author on every level of his personhood. His **"soul"** (inner man) was thirsting, and even his **"flesh"** (outer man) was aching with desire for his God. Certainly this is a far cry from the calm, detached kind of religion known by most churchmen today.

The Bible uses this kind of intense imagery over-and-again to identify the heart condition that believers ought to have in relation to the Savior. This language translates to mean, "I am famished! I am starving to know the Lord better." These words signal dissatisfaction with things as they are and an eager desire to go on and grow up in Christ. Notice that the psalmist confessed that his appetite for his God was predicated on the dryness of the spiritual climate around him. He said that he was living in **"a dry and thirsty land, where no water is."** In other words, it was the drought of dead religion and unanointed "church" that had awakened his discontentment with the status quo and driven him out of comfort-zone Christianity. One brother put it like this: "...dryness always leads to desperation. Out of their profound sense of dissatisfaction, often with a certain degree of gloom, people begin to cry out to God."[1] The man of God had begun to sense the awful spiritual vacuum of his day, and it had stirred within him a determination to have personal revival.

[1] Tom Phillips, *Revival Signs: The Coming Spiritual Awakening* (Gresham, Oregon: Vision House Publishing, Inc., 1995), pg. 213.

The primary condition for the arrival of real revival is the hunger and thirst of God's people for a closer walk with Him. Recall the words of Jesus in **Matthew 5:6**: **"Blessed are they which do hunger and thirst after righteousness: for they shall be filled."** This is restated in **Psalm 81:10** in words so simple even a child can understand: **"Open thy mouth wide, and I will fill it."** Dear ones, the matter of revival hinges on our willingness to get real about the dryness and deadness of our current condition. Out of that brutal honesty about the fact that we're in **"a dry and thirsty land, where no water is"** will grow a keen interest in a fresh manifestation of God Himself in our midst.

Furthermore, notice the psalmist's commitment to prioritize his seeking of the Lord: **"early will I seek Thee."** The phrase basically means, "Seeking God is at the top of my daily priorities." I don't mean to downplay the idea of early in the day, but the real sense of it is "highest on my list of daily concerns." In other words, when we begin to really long for the Lord, nothing will take precedence over seeking His face. Fellowship with God is the first thought of the morning, and it dominates everything else all day long. This is the eagerness for spiritual things that comes with the cultivation of a true appetite for God. Without a heart-hunger for the Lord, the things of the Spirit will get shouted down and shoved aside by the things of this world. But with a deep appetite for Christ, we will find it unthinkable that seeking Him should take second-place to anything or anyone.

2. The Essence of Spiritual Appetite.

What was it that particularly defined the psalmist's longing? He wrote that it was **"to see Thy power and Thy glory."** That is to say, this child of God was eaten up with a desire to see the living Lord manifest Himself. The old-time revival preachers spoke, wrote, and prayed about the "manifestation" of God. The history of spiritual awakening is marked by the use of such phrases as "the manifest presence of the Lord" and "the glory of God was manifest." One of the big differences between business-as-usual religion and genuine revival is the experiencing of the power and glory of God in the midst of His born again people. Brian Edwards made a careful study of the subject of revival and came to this conclusion: "If there is one aspect of worship today that is lacking, it is the felt presence of God. …In revival the presence of God becomes a tangible, felt experience."[1]

The foundational principle in spiritual appetite has to do with a deep desire **"to see"** God's power and glory displayed. It is a longing for a "God-consciousness" to pervade and prevail over the hearts of men and the atmosphere of the congregation. The term **"Thy power"** speaks of God's anointed activity; **"Thy glory"** speaks of His magnificent person. The **"power"** of God has to do with His mighty works; the **"glory"** of God has to do with His beautiful character. Spiritual appetite has this twin concern — that God would move in power and show up glory.

Please know that I am not speaking now of a carnal desire for spiritual entertainment. I'm not referring to a side-show mentality that just wants "church" to be more fun and exciting, so as to appeal to religious spectators who want an emotional thrill. In **James 4:2-3** the Word of God confronts two evils: first, the matter of failing to pray; but also, the issue of praying for something merely out of a desire to **"consume it upon your lusts."** Genuine spiritual appetite is not about a desire to appease the flesh, nor a longing for a religious "high" that scintillates my soul but leaves me still carnal and unrepentant. Hunger and thirst for the Lord really comes down to a desire that all flesh be brought to nothingness before the majesty of the Most High.

---

[1] Brian Edwards, *Revival! A People Saturated with God* (Darlington, Co. Durham, England: Evangelical Press, 1990), pg. 134.

Having an appetite for God is about a yearning to see God's power and glory. It's a desire for the Lord to show up in such a way that men may see what only He can do and who He really is. It is really a matter of becoming so sick and tired of seeing what man can do, and watching the parade of personalities and human programs, that you feel that you're just going to shrivel up and die if God Himself doesn't move in and take over in Holy Ghost revival. It is a yearning for the emptiness of man-made church to be replaced with the fullness of the King of glory.

3. The Expectation of Spiritual Appetite.

Here is what really drives the psalmist's spiritual quest: the expectation that true satisfaction can only be found in the Lord. Notice these key phrases from **Psalm 63**: **"Thy loving-kindness is better than life"** (vs. 3); **"my soul shall be satisfied as with marrow and fatness"** (vs. 5); and **"in the shadow of Thy wings will I rejoice"** (vs. 7). These statements combine to say that the reason the author was so hungry for the Lord was that he knew only a reviving move of God could really fill the aching void in his life. As long as we believe that satisfaction can be found somewhere else, we'll have a world of trouble consistently focusing on the Lord. But when we get a firm grip on the reality that God alone can satisfy our souls **"as with marrow and fatness,"** and that experiencing Christ in a manifest way **"is better than life,"** then we will inevitably begin to pant after the Lord.

There is not a man, woman or child who is not looking for something that will truly satisfy. All humans are in search of a source of **"marrow and fatness."** In the classic of early American literature entitled *Walden*, essayist Henry David Thoreau summarized the desire of all men:

I went to the woods because I wished to live desperately, to front only the essential facts of life, and see if I could learn what it had to teach, and not, when I came to die, discover that I had not lived. I did not wish to live what was not life, living is so dear... I wanted to live deep and suck all the marrow of life, to live so sturdily and Spartan-like as to put to rout all that was not life...[1]

Those are the words of an unconverted man, but they reflect something that is universal in the hearts of us all. We want life to be fulfilling and abundant. We don't want to just survive, to just muddle along in mild misery until one day we die. All of us — lost and saved, carnal and spiritual — desire soul satisfaction. The problem is that many, even within the ranks of Christianity, think that **"marrow and fatness"** can be found in material things and worldly involvements. However, Scripture couldn't be any clearer on this point — only the manifest fullness of God can give us that for which we're truly longing.

> **In the last day, that great day of the feast, Jesus stood and cried, saying, If any man thirst, let him come unto Me, and drink. [38] He that believeth on Me, as the scripture hath said, out of his belly shall flow rivers of living water. [39] (But this spake He of the Spirit, which they that believe on Him should receive: for the Holy Ghost was not yet given; because that Jesus was not yet glorified.) (John 7:37-39)**

Where do you expect to find satisfaction? Where do you turn

---

[1] *The Norton Anthology of American Literature* (New York: W.W. Norton & Co., Inc., 1979), pg. 1588.

to find **"marrow and fatness,"** to seek that which makes life worth living? That is the true revelation of your spiritual appetite.

The reality is that the only thing which can really satisfy any of us long-term is the power and glory of God. Understanding this is what drives believers who have salvation-sense to prioritize seeking God early (**"early will I seek Thee,"** vs. 1), and late (**"when I remember Thee upon my bed, and meditate on Thee in the night watches,"** vs. 6), and all through the day. When we finally realize that experiencing His **"lovingkindness is better than life"** (**vs. 3**), and that only in the shadow of His wings can true joy be found (**vs. 7**), then we will become people possessed with a passion to walk daily in revival. John Piper has written one of the most compelling statements in Christian literature: "God is most glorified in us when we are most satisfied in Him."[1] One of the big lessons of **Psalm 63** is that only in the Lord can we ever really find soul satisfaction, and this understanding then fuels our seeking Him for personal revival.

4. The Energy of Spiritual Appetite.

In **verse 8** the psalmist crystallized his personal commitment like this: **"My soul followeth hard after Thee."** How could it be put any better? The Hebrew verb translated **"followeth hard"** comes from a root word that means to overtake someone and then cling to them. It speaks of the determined pursuit of a goal, but also the commitment to maintain once the goal is achieved. It is an energetic word, full of zeal and fervency. Here are a couple of passages that reflect the same idea:

> **I stretch forth my hands unto Thee: my soul thirsteth after Thee, as a thirsty land. (Psalm 143:6)**

[1] John Piper, *A Hunger for God* (Wheaton, Ill.: Crossway Books, 1997), pg. 181.

**Yea, in the way of Thy judgments, O LORD, have we
waited for Thee; the desire of our soul is to Thy name,
and to the remembrance of Thee. [9] With my soul have
I desired Thee in the night; yea, with my spirit within
me will I seek Thee early: for when Thy judgments
are in the earth, the inhabitants of the world will
learn righteousness. (Isaiah 26:8-9)**

Spiritual appetite for God naturally produces the
energy we need to seek hard after Him. Many would perhaps
say, "I wish I could have revival, but I'm a tired man. I've got
a lot on my plate, and I just don't have enough time or energy
to seek God like I should." But the fact is that it is our very
appetite for the Lord that provides us with the motivation and
energy to prioritize seeking Him. To have no energy to seek
the Lord is to admit to having very little appetite for Him.
Apathy results in dull, listless religion; appetite produces
energetic followers after God.

We generally find the energy to do what we really want
to do. Our real appetites are always revealed by what we're
willing to expend energy in pursuing. This is one of the
reasons that the earthy images of hunger and thirst are used to
describe this highest and noblest attitude of the Christian to
his God—because physical appetite eventually reaches the
point of single-minded desperation. It refuses to be ignored,
and it can't be distracted by other things. It shouts for
attention and clamors to be fed and filled.

Another reason these terms are so important to
understanding the way of revival is that hunger and thirst are
constantly reoccurring. You may eat and drink till you can
hold no more at breakfast, but before the day is over you'll be
looking for another meal. That is why the psalmist spoke of
his commitment to "follow hard" after the Lord—not just
chasing Him down, but clinging to Him once all was on the
altar and the fire of revival had fallen. We need more than a

one-time "zap;" we need to surrender to a life-long passion for the nearness of God that begins fresh every day. Spiritual appetite fills us with the energy we need to follow on to know the Lord, to continually count all things as loss for the excellency of experiencing Jesus in intimate ways, to keep on pressing toward the prize of the high calling of God in Christ.

Is there any hope for a spiritual awakening in our day? Is there any hope for revival to break out in our land? If there is, it simply comes down to this: that we individually begin to be dissatisfied with where we are and begin to ache in our souls to see God move in power among us and manifest His glory to us. That would translate to mean that the biggest issue any of us can face is the question of our personal appetite for God. This is where we must begin in addressing the spiritual problems facing us; "Am I hungry and thirsty for my Lord?" If we can begin nowhere else, we all could at least start by confessing, "Lord, you know I'm not longing for You as I should, but I long to learn how to long. I'm hungry and thirsty to begin to be hungry and thirsty for Thee." I believe the God of all grace will honor that honest and humble beginning by fanning the flame of our passion until we're fully on fire for Him. And that is what revival is all about.

Chapter Six

True Spirituality

The words of Jesus from **Luke 6:20-26** form the basis for this chapter:

> And He lifted up His eyes on His disciples, and said, Blessed be ye poor: for yours is the kingdom of God. [21]Blessed are ye that hunger now: for ye shall be filled. Blessed are ye that weep now: for ye shall laugh. [22]Blessed are ye, when men shall hate you, and when they shall separate you from their company, and shall reproach you, and cast out your name as evil, for the Son of man's sake. [23]Rejoice ye in that day, and leap for joy: for, behold, your reward is great in heaven: for in the like manner did their fathers unto the prophets. [24] But woe unto you that are rich! for ye have received your consolation. [25]Woe unto you that are full! for ye shall hunger. Woe unto you that laugh now! for ye shall mourn and weep. [26] Woe unto you, when all men shall speak well of you! for so did their fathers to the false prophets.

It's important to understand from the outset that the Lord addressed these words to **"His disciples,"** as the opening phrase above indicates. This was a message from Jesus to His followers. Here are principles that Christians are to take to heart and use to orient our lives in accordance with the mind of Christ.

It is astonishing to see how radically the Lord Jesus reverses everything that the natural world assumes to be true and obvious. The "blessings" and "woes" pronounced in this text are exactly the opposite of what would be expected. When the world, and even much of the church world, thinks of someone as **"blessed,"** they certainly don't identify it with things like being poor, hungry, weeping, and despised. And on the other side of the issue, most wouldn't consider it a **"woe"** to be wealthy, full, laughing, and well-liked. When taken seriously, these words of Christ are quite shocking.

The terms **"blessed"** and **"woe"** are ancient prophetic devices that go back to the oldest books of the Bible as ways of crystallizing the way the Christian life is to be lived. **"Blessed"** basically means, "O, how well you're doing," and a **"woe"** is a serious statement of God's displeasure that brings judgment in its wake. You find this kind of summation in the preaching of Moses:

> **Behold, I set before you this day a blessing and a curse;** [27] **A blessing, if ye obey the commandments of the LORD your God, which I command you this day:** [28] **And a curse, if ye will not obey the commandments of the LORD your God, but turn aside out of the way which I command you this day, to go after other gods, which ye have not known.**

The Lord Jesus preached in the same vein, illustrating that there are two competing options available to **"His disciples"**—the way of blessing and the way of woe. The text asks in essence, "Do you want to get on well as a believer in Jesus? Are you interested in learning how to succeed in matters of eternal significance?" This is really what is at stake in this text. The Savior gives four basic points of inspection which we can use to take a personal inventory of our individual spirituality.

Some may wonder what this chapter has to do specifically with the subject of revival and spiritual awakening. My answer is, much in every way. Firstly, the word "revival" speaks of coming back to the place of full consciousness and vigorous life. To be revived is to be brought back up to the biblical standard of spiritual normality.

Dr. Lewis Drummond expressed it like this; "Revival simply moves God's people to become fully New Testament in theology and practice. ...A spiritual awakening can be summed up as inculcating into the very fabric of the church normal New Testament Christianity."[1] That being the case, what could be more profitable than a careful look into what Christ taught as "normal spirituality?" Secondly, a study into these things makes it obvious that they form a description of the kind of disciple who can be used of God to spark revival in the church.

What kind of Christian will God be able to use as a catalyst of change, a prayer warrior for awakening and spiritual renewal? This **Luke 6** text answers with four clear principles. It is paradoxical that what we might call "the keys to revival" and "the essence of revival" are identical. That is to say, when a disciple is fully set on seeking God for revival, and is meeting God's conditions for the coming of revival, then he is already revived, and is in fact fully awake and functional in the Body of Christ, able now to be an influence for revival in the congregation of the saints.

Consider these four points of inspection as they help us identify the difference between true and false spirituality, between that which is deep and authentic and that which is shallow and sham.

1. Blessed Are the Bankrupt.

THE CONDITION: vs. 20, "Blessed be ye poor: for yours is the kingdom of God."

The word **"poor"** is not being used here in reference to

[1] Lewis Drummond, *Eight Keys to Biblical Revival* (Minneapolis, Minnesota: Bethany House Publishers, 1994), pg. 147.

financial issues. This is a spiritual matter, as is obvious from a comparison with the parallel text of **Matthew 5:3**: **"Blessed are the poor in spirit; for theirs is the kingdom of heaven."** To be **"poor"** in the sense that Jesus is using the word is a matter of humility of spirit which grows out of an honest recognition of my deep neediness before God. Basically, Jesus taught, "Happy is the disciple who knows himself to be spiritually destitute and desperately needy before Me."

The "poverty" that invites the blessing of the Lord is the recognition of personal spiritual bankruptcy which admits that on my own I am totally insufficient and unable to do anything for the glory of God. Here is one who says, "I turned my pockets inside out, and found that I am flat broke when it comes to the personal power to be holy and God-honoring." The Old Testament prophet put it like this: **"we are all as an unclean thing, and all our righteousnesses are as filthy rags; and we all do fade as a leaf; and our iniquities, like the wind, have taken us away."**[1] You see, it is not just our sins that are as filthy rags before Holy God, but even **"our righteousnesses"** are contaminated and unclean.

In the sense of this teaching, being **"poor"** means that I am realistic about my insufficiency in the spiritual realm, and my total dependence on the grace of God for even the smallest advances toward godliness. Here is a quote from a brother who summed it up well: "There is no truth so neglected and yet so necessary to man's understanding of himself as the doctrine of man's fallen and depraved nature. Self-esteem teachings not-withstanding, man *deserves* a poor self-image. He is a poor self!"[2]

It must be said that this is certainly not about any whining kind of self-pity ("poor, poor, pitiful me"). It is simply the healthy honesty of **Romans 7:18**: **"I know that in**

---

[1] Isaiah 64:6

[2] Paul deParrie, *Satan's Seven-fold Schemes: An Overcomer's Guide to Spiritual Warfare* (Brentwood, TN: Wolgemuth & Hyatt, Publishers, Inc., 1991), pg. 122.

me (that is, in my flesh,) dwelleth no good thing: for to will is present with me; but how to perform that which is good I find not." This idea is directly reinforced by the very words of Jesus in **John 15:4-5**:

> **Abide in Me, and I in you. As the branch cannot bear fruit of itself, except it abide in the vine; no more can ye, except ye abide in Me. ⁵ I am the vine, ye are the branches: He that abideth in Me, and I in him, the same bringeth forth much fruit: for without Me ye can do nothing.**

It is very humbling to realize that what Christ needs from me — in order to use me to His glory — is not my strength and determination to do better for Him, but my realization of how weak and incapable I am on my own. What the Lord needs from me in order to bless and better use me is my understanding that without Him I can do nothing.

When I see myself as God's benefactor, thinking that without me doing my part His cause is bound to flounder, then I am not only clueless, but I'm in real spiritual danger. Christ is always the giver and I am always the beggar in absolute poverty before Him, so spiritually bankrupt that I can't even pay attention unless the Lord empowers me to do so. The fact is that even when I desire to serve and honor God, that very desire is derived from the operation of God's amazing grace in me.

> **...work out your own salvation with fear and trembling. For it is God which worketh in you both to will and to do of His good pleasure. (Philippians 2:12b-13)**

> **For I am the least of the apostles, that am not meet to be called an apostle, because I persecuted the church of God. ¹⁰ But by the grace of God I am what I am:**

and His grace which was bestowed upon me was not
in vain; but I laboured more abundantly than they all:
yet not I, but the grace of God which was with me.
(1 Corinthians 15:9-10)

The fact is that we all are so impoverished that left to
ourselves we can't even muster up a clean, honest desire to
live only for Him. My gracious God has to first work in me to
cause me even to want to know and do His good pleasure.

This is where everything spiritual begins: with the
humbling realization that I am "dead broke" and in constant
need of the grace of God to make any advance toward true
godliness, as well as to be of any use in regard to eternal
things. As strange as this sounds to the modern religious ear,
Christ taught that true spirituality is built upon the
foundation of total dependence on Him to be our source and
sufficiency.

THE CONSEQUENCE: vs. 20, "...for yours is the kingdom of
God."

The specific blessing that Jesus addressed to these
"poor" is the present-tense experience of kingdom life. In this
sense, **"the kingdom of God"** is used of something more than
just being converted to Christ, but living daily under His
Lordship. This is about **Matthew 6:33 ("Seek ye first the
kingdom of God, and His righteousness")** and **Romans 14:17
("For the kingdom of God is not meat and drink, but
righteousness, peace, and joy in the Holy Ghost.")**.

It makes sound biblical sense that when any disciple
begins to own up to his personal insufficiency and yield
himself to Christ's All-sufficiency, then the kingdom rule of
Jesus begins to be a day-by-day reality. Only after we have
been brought through the painful process of learning how
bankrupt we really are, and we have come to trust that Christ
is ALL we need, are we ready and willing to put ourselves

79

totally at His disposal. That's when His kingly reign begins to really manifest in us and through us, making us into **"ambassadors for Christ."**[1] It is here that the disciple starts to live from the perspective, "I am nothing; my King is everything. I am the ever-needy one; He is the all-sufficient One. I draw my life from Him, and I want only to have His abundant life flowing freely into and through me to the glory of God the Father." Then comes the victorious confession of the apostle Paul, **"Not that we are sufficient of ourselves to think anything as of ourselves; but our sufficiency is of God; Who also hath made us able ministers of the new testament."**[2]

THE CONTRAST: **vs. 24, "But woe unto you that are rich! for ye have received your consolation."**

When you understand the word **"poor"** to be spiritual in nature, speaking specifically of an honest recognition of insufficiency and neediness before the Lord, then you see that being **"rich"** is at root an attitude of arrogance and assumed self-sufficiency. There is no better illustration of this than **Revelation 3:15-17**:

> **I know thy works, that thou art neither cold nor hot: I would thou wert cold or hot.** [16] **So then because thou art lukewarm, and neither cold nor hot, I will spue thee out of My mouth.** [17] **Because thou sayest, I am rich, and increased with goods, and have need of nothing; and knowest not that thou art wretched, and miserable, and poor, and blind, and naked:**

---

[1] 2 Corinthians 5:20

[2] 2 Corinthians 3:5-6a

Christ Jesus addressed those words to a backslidden, lukewarm congregation of professing Christians who, like so many in our own day, desperately needed to have revival.

To be **"rich"** is to harbor a deceived attitude of self-reliance that says, "I'm doing just fine like I am; in fact, better than most." These **"rich"** feel no desperation for the emptying of self and the filling of the Spirit; they have no overwhelming sense that they absolutely must have Jesus ruling over every part of them, manifesting Himself in and through them. Billy Graham wrote, "No man is more pathetic than he who is in great need and is not aware of it. ...The pitiable thing about the Pharisees was not so much their hypocrisy as it was their utter lack of knowledge of how poor they actually were in the sight of God."[1]

Whereas the **"poor"** confess that within their own humanity dwells no good thing, the **"rich"** embody the worst side of **Luke 18:9-14**:

> **And He spake this parable unto certain which trusted in themselves that they were righteous, and despised others: [10] Two men went up into the temple to pray; the one a Pharisee, and the other a publican. [11] The Pharisee stood and prayed thus with himself, God, I thank thee, that I am not as other men are, extortioners, unjust, adulterers, or even as this publican. [12] I fast twice in the week, I give tithes of all that I possess. [13] And the publican, standing afar off, would not lift up so much as his eyes unto heaven, but smote upon his breast, saying, God be merciful to me a sinner. [14] I tell you, this man went down to his house justified rather than the other: for every one that exalteth himself shall be abased; and he that humbleth himself shall be exalted.**

---

[1] Billy Graham, *The Secret of Happiness* (Waco, TX: Word Books, 1985), pg. 32.

In the wise words of David Swartz, "One cannot simultaneously be poor in spirit and full of self. …Blessed is the man who genuinely lives in light of the knowledge that apart from the grace of God he is nothing."[1]

Remember, these principles are intended as inspection points for self-examination. The question then is, which comes closer to expressing my own spiritual life? Do I see myself as nothing on my own, and consequently yield all to Christ to be my everything? Or, am I living as if I'm fairly capable, and thus content to "do the best I can" for Jesus? God help us to remember the penetrating truth of **Galatians 6:3**: **"For if a man think himself to be something, when he is nothing, he deceiveth himself."**

2. Blessed Are the Dissatisfied.

THE CONDITION: **vs. 21a, "Blessed are ye that hunger now:"**

Comparing spiritual things with spiritual, the Lord Jesus is obviously using the idea of **"hunger"** to speak of an inner longing for divine reality. This is the matter of an intense appetite for spiritual fullness. Again, the parallel statement in **Matthew 5:6** expands and explains it: **"Blessed are they which do hunger and thirst after righteousness: for they shall be filled."** The blessing is spoken over them which hunger for **"righteousness,"** which is basically defined as "rightness with God." True spirituality is characterized by a craving to be really right with the Lord.

One thing is clear in Scripture: human beings have no **"righteousness"** on our own. We have no inherent power to please God, no ability to be truly and purely right with Him out of the storehouse of our own resources. In fact, remember the strong words of **Isaiah 64:6**; **"...all our righteousnesses**

---

[1] David Swartz, *The Magnificent Obsession* (Colorado Springs, CO: NavPress, 1990), pg. 100.

are as filthy rags." As has been discussed in the previous section, even our best attempts at righteousness are soiled by sin. We must have Divine empowerment even to want to please God, much less to be able to do so.

This is what makes the Good News of Christ such good news! Jesus has lived, died, and risen in order to provide us with the **"righteousness"** we need to be right with God. The glad tidings are summed up in **2 Corinthians 5:21**: **"For He** (God the Father) **made Him** (God the Son) **to be sin for us, Who knew no sin; that we might be made the righteousness of God in Him** (Jesus)." The only righteousness we can and will ever have is His righteousness, attributed to us judicially and manifested in us as we yield our lives to Jesus. So, the **"hunger"** spoken of in our text is really a yearning to be filled up with Christ, so as to become a vessel unto honor that is suitable for the Master's use.

Hungering after righteousness is really hungering after Jesus — that is, yieldedness to Him and intimacy with Him — because Christ alone is our righteousness. Here is the testimony of Scripture:

> **But of Him are ye in Christ Jesus, who of God is made unto us wisdom, and righteousness, and sanctification, and redemption:** [31]**That, according as it is written, He that glorieth, let him glory in the Lord. (1 Corinthians 1:30-31)**

> **But what things were gain to me, those I counted loss for Christ.** [8] **Yea doubtless, and I count all things but loss for the excellency of the knowledge of Christ Jesus my Lord: for whom I have suffered the loss of all things, and do count them but dung, that I may win Christ,** [9] **And be found in Him, not having mine own righteousness, which is of the law, but that which is through the faith of Christ, the righteousness which is of God by faith:** [10] **That I may know Him,**

83

and the power of His resurrection, and the fellowship
of His sufferings, being made conformable unto His
death. (Philippians 3:7-10)

The Apostle Paul's hunger was not for some righteousness
that he could manufacture on his own by means of trying to
keep a set of rules and regulations. Paul knew that only in
Christ could true righteousness be found. Consequently,
Paul's whole heart and life was consumed with a desire to
know Jesus in His fullness, so that the righteousness of Christ
could take him over. And that is exactly what the **"hunger"** of
Luke 6:21 is about—whole-hearted desire for a closer walk
with Jesus, a greater intimacy with God, and a renewed filling
of the Spirit. True spirituality will always involve this element
of intense hunger for the fullness of God.

THE CONSEQUENCE: **vs. 21, "Blessed are ye that hunger now:
for ye shall be filled."**

Jesus promised that the hungry shall be **"filled,"** and
that is a promise on which we can afford to stand. The fact is
that we will always be filled to the level of our heart-hunger
for God. Our experience of the righteousness and fullness of
Christ will always be determined by our inner yearning to
really **"know"** Him in the sense of **Philippians 3:10** (quoted
above).

How can I really be filled with the Spirit? What must I
do to facilitate being emptied of me and filled with all the
fullness of God? In a word, hunger! In a sentence, want Him
with desperate abandon! Augustine wrote, "God thirsts to be
thirsted after."[1] The Lord always responds to our appetite for
Him. When we want Him deeply and desperately, like a
starving man craves food and drink, then God gives Himself

---

[1] As quoted by Richard J. Foster, *Prayer: Finding the Heart's True Home* (San
Francisco, CA: HarperSanFrancisco, 1992), pg. 85.

to us. When we are indifferent and uninterested in being filled with Him and empowered by His righteousness, then He does not force His fullness upon us. Read it from the witness of the Bible itself:

> Thus saith the LORD that made thee, and formed thee from the womb, which will help thee; Fear not, O Jacob, my servant; and thou, Jesurun, whom I have chosen. [3] For I will pour water upon him that is thirsty, and floods upon the dry ground: I will pour My Spirit upon thy seed, and My blessing upon thine offspring: (Isaiah 44:2-3)

> Oh that men would praise the LORD for His goodness, and for His wonderful works to the children of men! [9] For He satisfieth the longing soul, and filleth the hungry soul with goodness. (Psalm 107:8-9)

> And ye shall seek Me, and find Me, when ye shall search for Me with all your heart. [14] And I will be found of you, saith the LORD: (Jeremiah 29:13-14a)

> And I say unto you, Ask, and it shall be given you; seek, and ye shall find; knock, and it shall be opened unto you. [10] For every one that asketh receiveth; and he that seeketh findeth; and to him that knocketh it shall be opened. [11] If a son shall ask bread of any of you that is a father, will he give him a stone? Or if he ask a fish, will he for a fish give him a serpent? [12] Or if he shall ask an egg, will he offer him a scorpion? [13]If ye then, being evil, know how to give good gifts unto your children: how much more shall your heavenly Father give the Holy Spirit to them that ask Him? (Luke 11:9-13)

Draw nigh to God, and He will draw nigh to thee. (James 4:8)

These verses sum up the message of the whole Bible, that God will bless any hungry soul with the greatest gift of all—Himself!

THE CONTRAST: **vs. 25a, "Woe unto you that are full! for ye shall hunger."**

In this context, to be **"full"** is to be content with your present level of religious life and to have no real passion for increased intimacy with the Lord. Again, the negative example of the Laodicean Church in **Revelation 3:17** says it all; **"I...have need of nothing."** Of course, that wasn't true; they had need of a great deal. They desperately needed revival and a fresh filling of the Holy Spirit. But they didn't think so; they were complacently comfortable just as they were.

It's shocking how easily we can be seduced into a carnal satisfaction with less than God's intended fullness. Many church folks get more upset over poor service at a restaurant on Sunday afternoon than they do over the absence of the power and glory of God in the Sunday morning worship service. Multitudes of backslidden believers are as stagnant as an old pond—and seemingly satisfied to have it that way! To be **"full"** is to be deluded and self-deceived, because the one who feels himself **"full"** is in reality the emptiest of all—so empty that he doesn't have sense enough to even recognize it as emptiness. Like Samson of old, he knows not **"that the Lord [is] departed from him."**[1]

Here again we must pause and use these words of Christ as a tool for self-examination. Which of these two

---

[1] See Judges 16:20.

conditions more closely resembles me? Am I personally hungry, marked by a gnawing appetite to go further with God into the death of self and the filling of the Spirit? Am I marked by a perpetual longing that Jesus might increase in me and that I might decrease? Or, am I full of myself, spiritually stagnant and content to have it so?

3. Blessed Are the Burdened.

<u>THE CONDITION:</u> **vs. 21b, "Blessed are ye that weep now:"**

Again, this must be understood in spiritual terms, and in the flow of the previous two principles. "Weeping" speaks of an attitude of contrition and brokenness over sin. **Matthew 5:4** is the parallel: **"Blessed are they that mourn: for they shall be comforted."** Surely this is that which is spoken of in **Psalm 51:17, "The sacrifices of God are a broken spirit: a broken and a contrite heart, O God, Thou wilt not despise."**
There is a logical progression to these first three tracks of truth. Honesty about our personal impoverishment will always leads to desperation for the filling of the Lord, which in turn produces brokenness over any and all sin. Specifically, we come to hate and grieve over anything and everything that hinders the Savior from having His way in us. The Apostle James described the process like this:

> **Draw nigh to God, and He will draw nigh to you. Cleanse your hands, ye sinners; and purify your hearts, ye double minded. [9] Be afflicted, and mourn, and weep: let your laughter be turned to mourning, and your joy to heaviness. (James 4:8-9)**

Initially, this mourning has to do with one's own sin, and it is the key ingredient to repentance, which results in

---

personal deliverance from my satanic strongholds. But this weeping goes much further than simply being concerned over my individual spiritual condition. Once a Christian is emptied out of self-rule and filled with the Spirit of God, then that believer begins to sense and share the burden of the Lord concerning the sub-normality of His backslidden church. The author of the spiritual classic, *Praying Hyde*, wrote this in his introduction: "The closer we draw to [God's] heart, the more we share His sorrows. It is not our broken heart we need, it is God's we need."[1]

When we touch the heart of God and allow Him to fill us with His Spirit, then whenever and wherever He is quenched and grieved, we will share His heartache. All who press on to know the Lord will discover the truth of these remarks from the great preacher and author A.W. Tozer:

> I would say to you who are wondering about the Spirit-filled life: If you just want to be happy, and nothing else, you had better steer away from the Spirit-filled life. The same Holy Spirit who will give you joy will also allow you to share His burdens and griefs.[2]

In **Ezekiel 8-11** there is a record of an extended vision given by the Lord to His prophet concerning the awful spiritual condition of the Old Testament people of God. Terrible carnality and idolatry were afoot in the very ranks of the house-hold of faith, and the glory of God was moving slowly away from them as a result. In the midst of that spiritual devastation, God gave instructions to a man with pen and ink to **"set a mark upon the foreheads of the men that sigh and that cry for all the abominations that be done in the midst**

---

[1] Francis McGaw, *Praying Hyde* (South Plainfield, NJ: Bridge Publishing, Inc., 1982), pg. 35.

[2] A.W. Tozer, *Rut, Rot or Revival* (Camp Hill, PA: Christian Publications, 1992), pg. 90.

thereof,"[1] who then were to be spared the judgment of death that was passing upon the inhabitants of Jerusalem. Weeping out of a burden over the waywardness of the corporate people of God was the one thing separating the blessed from the cursed.

If the questions are asked, "Who cares if revival comes? Who cares about spiritual awakening in the church today?" — then you and I must be able to honestly answer, "I do!" We so need a touch of the spirituality of the prophet Jeremiah at a time like this:

> **But if ye will not hear it, my soul shall weep in secret places for your pride; and mine eye shall weep sore, and run down with tears, because the LORD'S flock is carried away captive. (Jeremiah 13:17)**

THE CONSEQUENCE: **vs. 21b, "Blessed are ye that weep now: for ye shall laugh."**

In the short term there's nothing "hip" or "cool" about weeping. It's certainly not being touted as the hot new fad in how to "do church." But there's more to true spirituality than short-term amusement and light and fluffy entertainment. For those willing to invest in the deeper work of God, willing to embrace humility and burden over the serious sin issues that are at hand, the Lord has a long-term promise worth noting. The Old Testament expresses it beautifully:

> **For thus saith the high and lofty One that inhabiteth eternity, whose name is Holy; I dwell in the high and holy place, with him also that is of a contrite and humble spirit, to revive the spirit of the humble, and to revive the heart of the contrite ones. (Isaiah 57:15)**

---

[1] Ezekiel 9:4

They that sow in tears shall reap in joy. [6] He that goeth forth and weepeth, bearing precious seed, shall doubtless come again with rejoicing, bringing his sheaves with him. (Psalm 126:5-6)

True spirituality always involves brokenness before God, and out of that attitude of concern and contrition develops the godly sorrow that turns into Holy Ghost revival.

In every case, you can trace the great circumstances of those revivals back to their origins. You will always find that they had their births with one or more individuals in prayer, totally broken before God. Through intercession, under the weight of the sin of that nation, city, church, or a burden for another individual, God fell in Power.[1]

The brokenness itself is not the goal, but it is necessary to reach the goal. Weeping with a burden over sin leads to revival, and revival always results in fresh joy in the Lord. **Psalm 85:6** says, **"Wilt Thou not revive us again, that Thy people may rejoice in Thee?"** Spiritual burden is the bridge from where we are (impoverished and hungry) to where we need to be (filled afresh with the righteousness and gladness of Jesus).

THE CONTRAST: **vs. 25b, "Woe unto you that laugh now! For ye shall mourn and weep."**

If weeping here represents an attitude of spiritual burden and deep concern, then laughing is used to speak of spiritual insensitivity and careless foolishness. Billy Graham wrote, "The opposite of mourning is insensitivity, lack of

---

[1] Mickey Bonner, *Brokenness: The Forgotten Factor in Prayer* (Houston, TX: Mickey Bonner Evangelistic Association, 1994), pg. 143.

caring, unconcern, callousness, indifference."[1]   **"Woe"** is pronounced on those who are flippant and given over to carnal amusements.   In Ezekiel's vision, mentioned earlier in the chapter, the price tag was death for lack of tears over the sorry spiritual situation at hand:

> **And the LORD said unto him, Go through the midst of the city, through the midst of Jerusalem, and set a mark upon the foreheads of the men that sigh and that cry for all the abominations that be done in the midst thereof. [5] And to the others He said in mine hearing, Go ye after him through the city, and smite: let not your eye spare, neither have ye pity: [6] Slay utterly old and young, both maids, and little children, and women: but come not near any man upon whom is the mark; and begin at My sanctuary. Then they began at the ancient men which were before the house. (Ezekiel 9:4-6)**

There is a similar emphasis found in **Isaiah 22:12-14**:

> **And in that day did the Lord GOD of hosts call to weeping, and to mourning, and to baldness, and to girding with sackcloth: [13] And behold joy and gladness, slaying oxen, and killing sheep, eating flesh, and drinking wine: let us eat and drink; for to morrow we shall die. [14] And it was revealed in mine ears by the LORD of hosts, Surely this iniquity shall not be purged from you till ye die, saith the Lord GOD of hosts.**

It is not necessarily a sign of blessing to be dry-eyed and jovial. Sometimes it is a sign of **"woe,"** a sign of spiritual ignorance and insensitivity, an indicator that we are far from the heart of Jesus and have no idea what is really going on

[1] Billy Graham, *The Secret of Happiness* (Waco, TX: Word Publishing, 1985), pg. 49.

from the perspective of eternity. God forgive our coldness of heart, our apathy and indifference, our entertainment-loving, comfort-worshipping religious carnality. Frivolity, silliness, and irreverence must be replaced with deepest respect for the Lord, hatred of sin, and a burden for true revival to the glory of God.

What does this point of inspection do for you? I heard of a pastor who asked one of his most faithful men if he knew what the two greatest problems were in their church. The man's response was, "Pastor, I don't know, and I don't care!" After a moment's thought, the pastor answered, "You're exactly right. Our two greatest problems are that most of don't know where we stand with the Lord, and we don't much care." That comes too close to the truth for many of us. But true spirituality will always be characterized by concern — even to the point of weeping with the very burden of the Lord over the sinful sub-normality of His people.

4. Blessed Are the Despised.

THE CONDITION: **vs. 22, "Blessed are ye, when men shall hate you, and when they shall separate you from their company, and shall reproach you, and cast out your name as evil, for the Son of man's sake."**

This principle is different from the previous three in that it is not causative, but consequential. That is to say, the truly spiritual disciple does not seek to be persecuted, but, as a result of being truly spiritual, persecution is sure to come. Being hated, misunderstood, resented, maligned and shunned are strange companions to the word **"blessed"** (fortunate). The thing that marks such a one as blessed is not that the experiences themselves are pleasant or something to be sought out, but that these things indicate that here is a Christian who is standing true and standing in good company. **Verse 23** adds this important footnote to all of this: **"...for in like manner did their fathers unto the prophets."** True spirituality causes us to identify and company with those men and women of God who through the ages have stood for right and opposed idolatrous religion, including and culminating in the Lord Jesus Himself.

> **If the world hate you, ye know that it hated Me before it hated you. [19] If ye were of the world, the world would love his own: but because ye are not of the world, but I have chosen you out of the world, therefore the world hateth you. [20] Remember the word that I said unto you, The servant is not greater than his lord. If they have persecuted Me, they will also persecute you; if they have kept My saying, they will keep yours also. [21] But all these things will they do unto you for My name's sake, because they know not Him that sent Me. (John 15:18-21)**

True spirituality not only raises the resentment of the irreligious world; it also tends to offend and infuriate the carnal churchman and backslidden religious community. You may recall that pagan Pilate tried to release Jesus. It was the self-serving religious establishment, whose boat Christ had been rocking, that cried, **"Away with Him, crucify Him."** The Lord has no greater enemy than dead religion, and the truly godly have no greater abusers than the carnally religious. To pursue true spirituality is to ensure unpopularity with those of **2 Timothy 3:2-5**, who are **"lovers of their own selves...lovers of pleasures more than lovers of God; having a form of godliness, but denying the power thereof."** It is simply not possible to be well-pleasing to Holy God and at the same time be well-liked by those who have no real interest in holiness or godliness.

One thing is sure: each of Christ's disciples must decide whether we want most of all to be approved of God or of men—because it simply can't be both ways. Paul made it clear in **Galatians 1:10: "...Do I seek to please men? For if I yet pleased men, I should not be the servant of Christ."** Jeremiah was given this strong exhortation from the Lord at the very outset of his prophetic ministry:

> **Thou therefore gird up thy loins, and arise, and speak unto them all that I command thee: be not dismayed at their faces, lest I confound thee before them. [18] For, behold, I have made thee this day a defenced city, and an iron pillar, and brazen walls against the whole land, against the kings of Judah, against the princes thereof, against the priests thereof, and against the people of the land. [19] And they shall fight against thee; but they shall not prevail against thee; for I am with thee, saith the LORD, to deliver thee. (Jeremiah 1:17-19)**

That's not to say that all men will dislike the truly spiritual disciple. There will be companions on life's road, others who are serving God also in humility of spirit, hungry for the filling of the Spirit, broken and spilled out for Christ. But they are the definite minority, even within the professing church.

THE CONSEQUENCE: **vs. 23, "Rejoice ye in that day, and leap for joy: for, behold, your reward is great in heaven: for in the like manner did their fathers unto the prophets."**

"Rejoice...leap for joy..."—because this world is not our home, we're just a-passing through! The truly spiritual know full well that we are strangers and pilgrims on this earth, and here we have no continuing city. We are headed for a Home whose Builder and Maker is God.[1]

---

[1] See Hebrews 11:8-10, 13-16.

The Spirit itself beareth witness with our spirit, that we are the children of God: [17] And if children, then heirs; heirs of God, and joint-heirs with Christ; if so be that we suffer with Him, that we may be also glorified together. [18] For I reckon that the sufferings of this present time are not worthy to be compared with the glory which shall be revealed in us. (Romans 8:16-18)

For which cause we faint not; but though our outward man perish, yet the inward man is renewed day by day. [17] For our light affliction, which is but for a moment, worketh for us a far more exceeding and eternal weight of glory; [18] While we look not at the things which are seen, but at the things which are not seen: for the things which are seen are temporal; but the things which are not seen are eternal. (2 Corinthians 4:16-18)

One day the spiritually-minded disciples of Christ will reap what has been sown, as will the rest of humanity. But for the truly spiritual, what a day of rejoicing that will be!

THE CONTRAST: vs. 26, "Woe unto you, when all men shall speak well of you! For so did their fathers of the false prophets."

How opposite these words of Jesus are from the natural man's perspective! Christ taught that when everyone likes us, we're in real spiritual trouble. In fact, we can only be lumped in the category of false prophet. The false prophets were guilty of a number of offenses against God, but the one thing that always bound them together was the soft-pedaling of their message to always comfort and never confront, and in so

95

doing, they served to encourage the rebellious children of Israel to continue in their backsliding. The false prophets of the Old Testament were not always out-and-out heretics as much as they were spiritual sissies.

> **Thus saith the LORD of hosts, Hearken not unto the words of the prophets that prophesy unto you: they make you vain: they speak a vision of their own heart, and not out of the mouth of the LORD. [17] They say still unto them that despise Me, The LORD hath said, Ye shall have peace; and they say unto every one that walketh after the imagination of his own heart, No evil shall come upon you. ...Behold, I am against them that prophesy false dreams, saith the LORD, and do tell them, and cause My people to err by their lies, and by their lightness... (Jeremiah 23:16-17, 32a)**

Everyone enjoys the light-hearted; those who never seem to be down, who are free from any oppressive seriousness or deep burden — that is, everyone but Jesus. By the same token, few people delight in the company of the poor, the hungry, the broken-hearted, and the stern-voiced prophet who dares to expose the brutal truth — but Jesus pronounced such to be **"blessed"** of God. A.W. Tozer wrote these words about Leonard Ravenhill:

> Such a man is not an easy companion. The professional evangelist who leaves the wrought-up meeting as soon as it is over to hie him to the most expensive restaurant to feast and crack jokes with his retainers will find this man something of an embarrassment, for he cannot turn off the burden of the Holy Ghost as one would turn off a faucet.[1]

---

[1] A.W. Tozer, in the Foreword to Leonard Ravenhill's *Why Revival Tarries* (Minneapolis, Minn.: Bethany House Publishers, 1990), pg. 12.

Once more, this raises a question for self-examination. Are you a crowd-pleaser, or a Christ-pleaser? John the Baptist made the religious establishment of his day acutely uncomfortable when he labeled them a **"generation of vipers,"**[1] but Jesus said of John that there was never a greater man born of woman.[2] When the last word on earth has been spoken, the last note of song sung, and the last mortal breath drawn, nothing will then matter except, "What does the Lord Jesus Christ think of me?" When all of His disciples appear before Him at the Judgment Seat of Christ, the only issue of relevance will be, "Was I numbered in the ranks of the false prophets, or did I stand in the gap and make up the hedge with the true servants of God?"

Search me, O God!

Here is the radical standard of true spirituality as taught by Jesus Himself. It is both the key to revival and the essence of revival. God grant us the courage to personally surrender to the searching of the Holy Spirit along these four critical inspection points. Is my personal spirituality deep and real, or shallow and sham? Remember that these things mean the difference between being **"blessed"** of God and being under His **"woe."**

---

[1] See Luke 3:7.

[2] Matthew 11:11.

Chapter Seven

Revival Preaching

There are few Old Testament chapters more beloved and well-used among those with a heart for revival than that of **1 Kings 18**. This thrilling passage records the story of the falling of the fire of God on the altar of sacrifice, and the dramatic triumph of the Truth over the lies of idolatry. Many a message has been preached from this text on the theme of "The Fire of Revival," and rightly so. In the context of this chapter, we find the prophet Elijah doing a number of significant things: he boldly challenged the false prophets of Baal, he rebuilt the altar of the Lord that had been allowed to fall into neglect and decay, he prepared a sacrifice according to biblical guidelines, and then he saturated it all with water so that when the fire fell only the true God could get glory for it. And when Elijah called out to the Lord in faith, heaven opened and fire came down! What a day that must have been, and how we ought to long for a spiritual reenactment of it in our own day.

Among the many things that are noteworthy in this delightful chapter, I'm going to focus attention on one little moment, when the man of God preached a single-sentence sermon to the people of Israel. In **1 Kings 18:21**, we find these words:

> **And Elijah came unto all the people, and said, "How long halt ye between two opinions? If the LORD be God, follow Him: but if Baal, then follow him." And the people answered him not a word.**

In this one-verse message there are several things that are noteworthy concerning the fundamental message of revival.

What kinds of things must be addressed to the people of God when spiritual awakening is the critical need of the hour? What ought we to be dealing with in our individual lives and corporate congregations at this point in Christian history, when our nation of churches so desperately needs the fire of God to fall and ignite revival in our midst?

There are three tracks of truth that stand out in this wonderful little text. I believe these things combine to form the pressing need in Christian preaching and thinking today.

1. *The Confrontation of Carnal Compromise.*

It's important to note that those addressed by Elijah in this brief message were not the false prophets of Baal, nor the wicked king and queen of Israel, but the rank and file of those called by the name of the Lord. Scripture uses the term **"all the people"** to identify Elijah's intended audience, and the phrase means "the throng, the public." The key word can even be rendered, "the family," indicating that this was the congregation of those who ostensibly were identified as the people of God. **"And Elijah came unto all the people, and said, 'How long halt ye between two opinions?'"**

It is this that makes revival necessary at any given point in Christian history — the professing people of God come to the place of halting between two opinions. In other words, believers begin to be spiritually indecisive and wishy-washy in their attitudes and actions because of carnality and worldliness, which results in spiritual compromise and moral cowardice. The word **"halt"** literally means "to vacillate, to bounce around between two things." It has the sense of hopping from foot to foot, and is one of the Hebrew words used of dancing, which is very suggestive of what was going on. Those who were supposed to be the household of faith were dancing around the issue of who would really be Lord of their lives. One scholarly work uses the word "limp" in translating this Hebrew word[1], because the idea seems to be that the Israelites had bounced around on this issue so long that they were virtually crippled by the indecisiveness and worn out by trying to play both ends against the middle.

The message of revival is by definition confrontational. It calls God's people to account for the areas of our lives that are compromised with the false gods of this world, and it demands that we repent of all cowardice and indecision. At times of prevailing backsliding and worldliness, God's children choose to forget the essence of the true gospel. But when a revival preacher comes on the scene he always invokes this fundamental reminder:

> **The light of the body is the eye: if therefore thine eye be single, thy whole body shall be full of light. [23] But if thine eye be evil, thy whole body shall be full of darkness. If therefore the light that is in thee be darkness, how great is that darkness! [24] No man can serve two masters: for either he will hate the one, and love the other; or else he will hold to the one, and despise the other. Ye cannot serve God and mammon. (Matthew 6:22-24)**

Trying to dance around on this issue and find a way to be both Christian and worldly is to court moral insanity and become spiritually schizophrenic, and it can only end in ruin. In the strong words of **James 4:4, "Ye adulterers and adulteresses, know ye not that the friendship of the world is enmity with God? Whosoever therefore will be a friend of the world is the enemy of God."** Again, in **1 John 2:15** the Bible says, **"If any man love the world, the love of the Father is not in him."**

---

[1] C.F. Keil and F. Delitzsch, *Commentary on the Old Testament in Ten Volumes, Volume III* (Grand Rapids, Michigan: William B. Eerdmans Publishing Company, 1988), pg. 245.

The plain fact is that we can't have it both ways. Baal and Jehovah can't both be God in my life, and to refuse to take a clear stand on the matter is still to take a stand — against full surrender to the only One who deserves the title Lord of all. Jesus preached, **"He that is not with Me is against Me,"**[1] indicating that anything less that total commitment to Him is full-on rebellion against Him. In that same vein, the prophet of revival came preaching a message of confrontation to Israel, demanding that they recognize and reckon with their falseness and foolishness in trying to serve two masters.

If you think that this problem evaporated with the generations of Israel in the Old Testament then you are not paying much attention to the modern church world. There's not a Christian community in this land that is not facing a tidal wave of worldliness and carnal compromise in its membership. Multitudes claim to know and love Jesus, yet they live such a double-minded kind of "spirituality" that they are virtually indistinguishable from the unconverted world around them. Like the lyrics to a country song I heard over the loudspeakers of a convenience store, many a modern church member wants a six-pack of beer on Saturday night, and "Amazing Grace" on Sunday morning. But the truth about God's amazing grace is found in **Titus 2:11-14**:

> **For the grace of God that bringeth salvation hath appeared to all men, 12 Teaching us that, denying ungodliness and worldly lusts, we should live soberly, righteously, and godly, in this present world; 13 Looking for that blessed hope, and the glorious appearing of the great God and our Saviour Jesus Christ; 14 Who gave Himself for us, that He might redeem us from all iniquity, and purify unto Himself a peculiar people, zealous of good works.**

---

[1] Matthew 12:30

On any given Sunday morning, church pews across this land are filled with people who profess to be worshippers of God, who just the night before were going places and doing things that so grieve the heart of Jesus that it would have to be called anti-Christ. Like those of **Titus 1:16, "They profess that they know God, but in works they deny Him, being abominable, and disobedient, and unto every good work reprobate."** Whereas the true gospel calls the born again to **"love the Lord thy God with all thy heart, and with all thy soul, and with all thy mind, and with all thy strength,"**[1] the mood of the day seems to be more in keeping with **2 Timothy 3:1, 4 — "men shall be lovers of their own selves...lovers of pleasures more than lovers of God."**

The real tragedy is that the one most hurt by this kind of foolishness is the compromiser himself. **James 1:8** states that **"the double minded man is unstable in all his ways."** Furthermore, **James 4:7-8** records this by way of exhortation: **"Submit yourselves therefore to God. Resist the devil, and he will flee from you. Draw nigh to God, and He will draw nigh to you. Cleanse your hands, ye sinners; and purify your hearts, ye double minded."** The double-minded believer is his own worst enemy, because he is attempting to submit both to God and the devil, and he is trying to resist both God and the devil at the same time. The result is total rebellion to the true message of Christianity and utter spiritual defeat of the compromiser.

2. The Call for Clear Commitment.

In the process of confronting Israel's indecisiveness, the man of God demanded that they take one side or the other. **"And Elijah came unto all the people, and said, 'How long halt ye between two opinions? If the LORD be God, follow**

---

[1] Mark 12:30

Him: but if Baal, then follow him.'" No more dancing around on this matter; no more bouncing back and forth—a clear commitment must be made. It has the ring of **Exodus 32:26** about it: **"Then Moses stood in the gate of the camp, and said, 'Who is on the LORD's side? Let him come unto me.'"** Moses' successor sounded the same note in **Joshua 24:15**: **"Choose you this day whom ye will serve; ...but as for me and my house, we will serve the LORD."**

The message of revival focuses on the absolute necessity of repentance from all forms of idolatry and fresh surrender to the Lordship of the Lord over every part of our lives. If the real heart of Christianity is loving our God with our all, then revival will always center in the born again repenting our way back to the place of a sold-out commitment to love the Lord with more than just some of our selves, or even most, but with our everything. That which makes revival needful is found in **Revelation 2:4**: **"I have somewhat against thee, because thou hast left thy first love."** And that which defines what revival really is can be found in **Matthew 4:10**: **"Thou shalt worship the Lord thy God, and Him only shalt thou serve."** It's that **"only"** that gives many of us so much trouble—not serve God also, but serve **"Him only."** Here it is from the ministry of the prophet Samuel:

> **...all the house of Israel lamented after the LORD.**
> **³And Samuel spake unto all the house of Israel, saying, If ye do return unto the LORD with all your hearts, then put away the strange gods and Ashtaroth from among you, and prepare your hearts unto the LORD, and serve Him only: and He will deliver you out of the hand of the Philistines. (1 Samuel 7:2b-3)**

As long as Jesus is just one of many priorities in our lives, and one of many loves in our hearts, we will always be a sorry spectacle and useless excuse for a Christian. Recall the pathetic description of the apathetic religionists in **2 Timothy**

3:4b-5: **"lovers of pleasures more than lovers of God; having a form of godliness, but denying the power thereof: from such turn away."** Just going through the motions of church; dead and powerless; consistently defeated by the world, the flesh and the devil; so distracted by the idolatry of the momentary that we never amount to anything of eternal value. God deliver us from it! In such an environment, God is robbed of the glory He is due, and the believer is robbed of the joy and peace that comes from whole-hearted surrender to Jesus. It is right here that the Word of the Lord comes, demanding that we clear away the clutter and get back to what it really means to be saved by grace — which is all-out love and obedience to Jesus Christ as Lord. God, in His great mercy and grace, sends the message of revival to His errant people, stirring up some faithful prophets to sound the alarm and call the believing community back to true commitment.

The message is so pointed that it actually implies that if we're not going to go all-out for Christ, then we need not bother going at all. Elijah preached, **"How long halt ye between two opinions? If the LORD be God, follow Him: but if Baal, then follow him."** He seems to say, "Pick one side or the other, but stop trying to serve both Jehovah and Baal as dual lords of your lives." Jesus Himself said as much in **Revelation 3:15-16**: **"I know thy works, that thou art neither cold nor hot: I would thou wert cold or hot. So then because thou art lukewarm, and neither cold nor hot, I will spue thee out of My mouth."** Better one way or the other than somewhere in the middle, muddling along in a kind of half-hearted "no man's land" of such spiritual mediocrity that no one can tell for sure what you really are. If you're going to be a worldling, then go on and be a heathen. But if you're going to claim to be a Christian, then come on and love Christ with all you are. Stop trying to straddle a non-existent fence. Quit being a religious schizophrenic. Get in or get out, but do something one way or the other.

3. The Charge for Complete Consecration.

When Elijah preached, **"If the LORD be God, follow Him: but if Baal, then follow him,"** he obviously was not implying that he was unsure as to which was true. Elijah knew who the one true God is. This word was a challenge to the people of Israel to put shoe leather to their profession of faith and actually **"follow"** the Lord in their lifestyle behavior. The word **"follow"** literally means "to go after" something or someone, as in **Psalm 63:8, "My soul followeth hard after Thee."** The word can also mean "to live or exist," and the idea is that if we really believe that Jehovah is God, then we ought to conduct ourselves with the realization that He alone is the reason we exist, and His glory is the goal of our living. Our actual lives, made up of our attitudes and actions, aren't to be parceled out between Jesus and the world, between God's will and self-will, between the Holy Spirit and unclean spirits. The Lord alone is to be the be-all and end-all of our existence.

The word **"follow"** carries the idea of making the True and Living God the one and only object of our passionate pursuit. This keenness of purpose is found in **Hebrews 12:1-2: "...let us lay aside every weight, and the sin which doth so easily beset us, and let us run with patience the race that is set before us, Looking unto Jesus the author and finisher of our faith..."** It answers the question, "What do I really want out of life?" with the clarion voice of consecration, "I just want the Lord! I only want to know Him and please Him well, and to give Him the glory He is due." One of my favorite hymns expresses it beautifully:

My goal is God Himself, not joy, nor peace,
Nor even blessing, but Himself, my God;
'Tis His to lead me there — not mine, but His —
At any cost, dear Lord, by any road.

So faith bounds forward to its goal in God,
And love can trust her Lord to lead her there;
Upheld by Him, my soul is following hard
Till God hath full fulfilled my deepest prayer.[1]

In this context of pursuing intimacy with God, the word **"follow"** also communicates the idea of willing submission to the leadership of the Lord in the practical details of life. In the words of the hymn above, "'Tis His to lead me there—not mine, but His." To **"follow"** the Lord is to actually go where He leads; to simply tag along behind Him and allow Him to blaze the trail. Jesus said, **"My sheep hear My voice, and I know them, and they follow Me"** (John 10:27), and, **"If any man will come after Me, let him deny himself, and take up his cross daily, and follow Me"** (Luke 9:23).

One thing is sure: informed disobedience to the known Word and will of God disqualifies us from being His followers. No one can be said to be following the Lord if we are aware of things in our lives that displease Him and we permit them to remain. Following Jesus means obedience to Him, and disobedience means that we're going our own way. This is made plain in **1 Samuel 15:22-23:**

> **And Samuel said, Hath the LORD as great delight in burnt offerings and sacrifices, as in obeying the voice of the LORD? Behold, to obey is better than sacrifice, and to hearken than the fat of rams. [23] For rebellion is as the sin of witchcraft, and stubbornness is as iniquity and idolatry.**

---

[1] Frances Brook, "My Goal Is God Himself," verses 1 and 2; www.hynmal.net.

If a second witness is needed, here are the words of Jesus Himself: **"He that hath My commandments, and keepeth them, he it is that loveth Me" (John 14:21**). So many church-goers claim that they truly love the Lord, but they make no serious effort to actually obey the principles of His Word. Many are indifferent to His commands, manifested by the fact that they give almost no time or effort to even reading His Word consistently to see what His commands are. And some are openly hostile to His commands, as evidenced by their angry reactions to any Bible preaching and teaching that contradicts their personal preferences and habits.

The message of revival is most needed at just such a time as this, calling the people of God back to the purity of our First Love. The charge of preaching for spiritual awakening always includes a challenge to actually **"follow"** the Lord of glory, and give Him the undiluted, uncompromising devotion and obedience that He deserves. For many years I have loved the call of **Psalm 96:8**: **"Give unto the Lord the glory due unto His name."** How is this possible? By means of **1 Corinthians 15:58**: **"Be ye steadfast, unmoveable, always abounding in the work of the Lord."**

Here it is in a nutshell—the difference between lackadaisical religion and red-hot revival. We must be willing to have our carnality confronted and our spiritual compromise called on the carpet. We must hear the call of the Lord to clear commitment to Him, and receive with meekness the challenge of the Spirit to order our conduct in the way of full consecration to His will and Word. May the Lord help that not one of us responds to God's prophetic message like those of our original text. According to **1 Kings 18:21**, after hearing Elijah's impassioned appeal, **"...the people answered him not a word."** What a shame, and what a way to guarantee disaster! Their spiritual cowardice remained in place, and their carnal religion left them bound and gagged in a silent betrayal of their Redeemer. The eventual result was that the people of Israel were carried away captive by a hateful enemy, and they never again knew the glory of the Lord that had once been upon them as the covenant people of God.

Dear family of faith, let us not allow the Word of the Lord to fall on deaf ears and unresponsive hearts. God help that we can each one give the correct response when the Lord sends one of His revival preachers our way:

I'll say yes, Lord, yes,
To your will and to your way;
I'll say yes, Lord, yes,
I will trust you and obey.
When your Spirit speaks to me
With my whole heart I'll agree,
And my answer will be yes, Lord, yes.[1]

---

[1] Lynn Keesecker, "Yes, Lord, Yes," © 1983, Manna Music, Inc.

Chapter Eight

A Heart for God

The **119ᵗʰ Psalm** is the longest single section of Scripture in our Bibles, made up of 176 verses. And the grand theme of them all is the irreplaceable importance of God's written Word in the hearts of His children. Spiritual awakening, as well as all spiritual growth, is dependent upon the operation of God's inspired Word in the yielded minds and lives of believers. No Christian book or literature is worth the paper it's printed on if it doesn't serve the purpose of calling the saints of God back to the Bible, and building its entire message on "thus saith the Lord." The reason that the chapters of this book have been tied directly to specific Bible texts is because nothing other than what Scripture has to say is of any real significance.

In light of that, I'm turning attention now to one section of **Psalm 119**, in order to identify how a revived Christian thinks and lives. Much of this book so far has been focused on passages in Scripture that point out the sin issues that must be addressed before revival can come. In this chapter, we will look into a text that illustrates what revival will do in terms of transforming the way Christians think, prioritize, and behave.

The **119ᵗʰ Psalm** is divided into 22 sections, each one introduced by a letter of the Hebrew alphabet. The portion on which we'll be focused is found in **verses 57-64**:

> **Thou art my portion, O LORD: I have said that I would keep Thy words.**
> **⁵⁸ I entreated Thy favour with my whole heart: be merciful unto me according to Thy word.**
> **⁵⁹ I thought on my ways, and turned my feet unto Thy testimonies. ⁶⁰ I made haste, and delayed not to keep Thy commandments.**

61 The bands of the wicked have robbed me: but I have not forgotten Thy law.
62 At midnight I will rise to give thanks unto Thee because of Thy righteous judgments.
63 I am a companion of all them that fear Thee, and of them that keep Thy precepts.
64 The earth, O LORD, is full of Thy mercy: teach me Thy statutes.

These are the words of a believer who really had a heart for God. The psalmist's passionate love for the Lord is expressed in four specific ways, and they point us to four particular spiritual principles that help illuminate the every-day life of a revived Christian.

It's very important to realize that revival is not just a momentary experience of sensational emotions or dramatic manifestations. True revival is a child of God coming back to full wakefulness, and then living on a level of biblical normalcy. The great preacher, Vance Havner, said, "We have been content with the subnormal for so long, however, that normal New Testament Christianity appears to most church members to be abnormal!"[1] We need more than a momentary eruption of spiritual fervor; we need to settle into a lifestyle of revived living. Here is a text that can help us to that end.

These eight verses naturally divide into four couplets, each of which informs us of an aspect of revived thinking and living. Although the psalmist is expressing his own commitment to the Lord, I will outline this text using the first person pronoun, because I want to make this personal to my own life.

---

[1] Vance Havner, *Living in Kingdom Come* (Westwood, NJ: Fleming H. Revell Co., 1967), pg. 84.

1. My Portion.

This tremendous section of Scripture begins with the man of God confessing that, as far as he was concerned, the Lord was all he needed and all he wanted. **"Thou art my portion, O LORD: I have said that I would keep Thy words."** Let others choose to live for what they will—material wealth, personal ambition, physical pleasure, hobbies and sports, self and sin, and whatever else—I choose the Lord as my reason for living. One dear brother put it like this: "…he was saying to the Lord, 'Thou art all I want. I am done with vanity.'"[1] This recalls the unmistakably clear words of **Joshua 24:14-15**:

> **Now therefore fear the LORD, and serve Him in sincerity and in truth: and put away the gods which your fathers served on the other side of the flood, and in Egypt; and serve ye the LORD. [15] And if it seem evil unto you to serve the LORD, choose you this day whom ye will serve; whether the gods which your fathers served that were on the other side of the flood, or the gods of the Amorites, in whose land ye dwell: but as for me and my house, we will serve the LORD.**

In essence, our text is the psalmist saying a hearty, "Amen!" to Joshua's commitment, and adding, "Me too!"

This is first of all about _FAITH_. To say, **"Thou art my portion, O LORD,"** is to have total confidence that He is enough, and indeed much more that I could ever even understand and appropriate. The revived saint, with a heart wholly given to the Lord, orders his mind and life with this understanding: "I don't need anything outside of Christ Jesus Himself to fulfill and satisfy me. The Lord alone is the Savior

---

[1] S. Franklin Logsdon, _Lest Ye Faint_ (Wheaton, Ill.: Bowdon Publications, 1965), pg. 146.

111

of my life, the strength of my soul, the joy and rejoicing of my heart. He is my all-in-all." Many modern "believers" cannot honestly say, **"The Lord is my portion,"** because they have no confidence that He is enough. I will change the pronoun purposely, because I face this tactic of the devil as much as anyone; often we are afraid to "limit" ourselves just to Jesus, which is why we struggle so with double mindedness. We have too much in common with those of **Jeremiah 2:13: "For My people have committed two evils; they have forsaken Me the fountain of living waters, and hewed them out cisterns, broken cisterns, that can hold no water."** It's so easy to be seduced by the devil and our own silly flesh into thinking that we must have something more than the Lord to make life full and happy. So, we wind up wasting our substance on vanity and foolishness while neglecting the one thing that would make life truly meaningful — namely, all-out surrender to the Lord as our portion.

This is also about _FOCUS_. In other words, we must make a settled choice to keep our eyes of faith concentrated on the greatness of our God, and thus keep ourselves centered on Him as the great reason for our existence. The questions could be asked on a theoretical level, "Have you any faith in God? Do you have any confidence that His Word is true and He is enough?" Most professing Christians would answer glibly, "Of course I do!" However, the true answer to those questions is not found in words spoken or decision cards signed, but in the priorities of life and the focus of our thoughts. The real questions are, "What are you living for? Where is your mind and heart focused — not just in times of crises and distress, but on an everyday, ordinary basis?"

> **I have set the LORD always before me: because He is at my right hand, I shall not be moved. [9] Therefore my heart is glad, and my glory rejoiceth: my flesh also shall rest in hope. (Psalm 16:8-9)**

Mine eyes are ever toward the LORD; for He shall pluck my feet out of the net. (Psalm 25:15)

There are dozens of things that compete to be the "portion" of our lives every day. You can always tell which one has the preeminence on the basis of that with which we are most obsessed. The right and healthy obsession is found in this text: **"Thou art my portion, O LORD: I have said that I would keep Thy words. I entreated Thy favour with my whole heart: be merciful unto me according to Thy word."**

2. My Pattern.

If the Lord is indeed our portion, then that will be reflected in a very specific pattern of life—and I mean by that the habit of our day-to-day thinking and living. **Verses 59-60** put in the simplest of terms:

> **I thought on my ways, and turned my feet unto Thy testimonies. I made haste, and delayed not to keep Thy commandments.**

This certainly is about cultivating a holy habit of <u>SELF-EXAMINATION</u>. The word **"ways"** speaks of a journey, a road being traveled, and then figuratively, the direction that my life is taking. The psalmist said, "I have taken, and continue to take, a hard, honest look at the direction that I'm moving spiritually." There is a sense here of an inventory going on.

Do you know that there aren't many who seriously do what this text talks about—at least not on a consistent basis? Most of us rush through life from one thing to the next, filling our days with ceaseless activity, never taking the time or trouble to ask the fundamental question, "Where is all of this taking me?" What about **"my ways?"** Is the direction that I'm moving right and godly, causing me to grow in the Lord, or distracting me from Him and promoting a backslidden life?

We in this nation and generation are in particular danger of being so distracted by the rush of life that we wind up totally unaware of our real spiritual condition. We even have a fancy word for it now — multi-tasking. One of the devil's chief tactics against us in this culture is to keep us so wound up and involved in momentary demands that we never take a serious look at our eternal souls. We seem to be afraid of silence and stillness. Our cell phones are never put down, our media inlets are rarely turned off, and we can barely focus on driving down the highway for 'tweeting' or texting. Our hands and heads are so full of sights and sounds that the still, small voice of the Holy Spirit just gets lost in the shuffle, because we are not intentional and aggressive enough to stop from time to time and just think on our ways.

Scripture repeatedly urges us to this kind of concentrated reflection, and warns that it is the only way to ensure spiritual health and well-being.

> **Let us search and try our ways, and turn again to the LORD. 41 Let us lift up our heart with our hands unto God in the heavens. (Lamentations 3:40-41)**

> **Now therefore thus saith the LORD of hosts; Consider your ways. (Haggai 1:5, 7)**

> **For if we would judge ourselves, we should not be judged. 32 But when we are judged, we are chastened of the Lord, that we should not be condemned with the world. (1 Corinthians 11:31-32)**

> **Examine yourselves, whether ye be in the faith; prove your own selves. Know ye not your own selves, how that Jesus Christ is in you, except ye be reprobates? (2 Corinthians 13:5)**

It is imperative that we each one make a point to cultivate the habit of self-awareness. Keep a close, cautious eye on your own heart-condition and direction of life. Don't just drift along with the current of the world. Think on your ways. Ask yourself tough questions from time to time about the way your life is heading. Otherwise, inevitably you will wind up distracted by the world and poured out on the altar of foolishness. One of my favorite hymns says,

> Prone to wander, Lord I feel it,
> Prone to leave the God I love.
> Here's my heart, O take and seal it,
> Seal it for Thy courts above.[1]

It is that "proneness to wander" that demands the concentrated attention and effort of our text: **"I thought on my ways, and turned my feet unto Thy testimonies."**

However, there is more to this than just a mental exercise. Also found here is the commitment to _SWIFT OBEDIENCE_. Having looked closely at my ways, I am then to turn **"my feet"** to the Word of God. Notice, not just turn my thoughts to the testimonies, but turn **"my feet"** — indicating the aligning of my real-life behavior with the teachings of the Bible. And I am to do so in an urgent manner. The psalmist put it like this:

> **I thought on my ways, and turned my feet unto Thy testimonies. I made haste, and delayed not to keep Thy commandments.**

For the wide-awake child of God who is living in a state of revival, the matter of obedience to the Word is no light

---

[1] Robert Robinson, "Come, Thou Fount of Every Blessing," *Baptist Hymnal* (Nashville, TN: Convention Press, 1956), pg. 313.

and trivial thing — certainly nothing over which we're to dawdle and hesitate. The intent seems to be, "I am determined to regularly think on my ways, and if I discover that I've drifted in some area from the Lord, I will not delay for one moment; I will run back to Him in fresh surrender unto obedience to His will and way." The maintenance of revival, going beyond just a church-service high to a lifestyle of awakened Christianity, is dependent on keeping a short sin list. That means, nothing that is not of God is allowed to fester or get a toe-hold; all disobedience and spiritual drift is dealt with instantly and without excuse.

I certainly get the sense that maintaining a right way and a close walk with the Lord was no religious game for the psalmist. He looked upon keeping his **"feet"** in the **"testimonies"** of God as the most urgently important matter in the world. This is a reflection of the deep reverence that this believer had for his Redeemer. You can always tell a great deal about a person's true heart for God on the basis of the urgency with which they approach the matter of repentance of known sin and surrender to obedience. If it's a very casual thing with you, such that you don't mind at all taking your own sweet time about it, delaying and excusing yourself as long as possible, dragging your feet and pulling back against the conviction of the Holy Spirit, then you have a bigger problem than the issue at hand. Where there is no urgency (**"haste"**) to obey God, then neither is there any real respect, fear, or love of Him. Whenever known sin is tolerated and taken lightly, it always means that the Lord is being taken lightly. When men have a low view of God, it causes them to have a high view of themselves, and a light view of sin.

Brothers and sisters in Christ, to live in revival we must cultivate the habit of taking the Lord seriously. We must urge our own hearts daily to recall, *This matter of living in obedience to God's Word is serious business, nothing to trifle with, requiring immediate and aggressive response as soon as I know there is a problem.* More vital than where I'm going to eat my next meal, or how I'm going to pay my bills, or how many more days I have to live on this earth, or anything else I can name or think, is the issue, *Am I really right with God? Are my feet walking in the way of His Word?* We must take time to think on this matter, to consider our ways in light of eternity. And if thinking on our **"ways"** causes us to come under conviction from the Lord that there are things that displease Him, let us **"make haste and delay not"** to surrender all to Him again and again, a hundred times a day if need be. Our merciful, gracious Father stands ready to forgive all sin and empower supernatural obedience through the resurrection victory of our Lord Jesus Christ— provided we will flee to Him in childlike faith.

3. My Praise.

This text reminds me that every Christian has wicked enemies who attack us mercilessly: **verse 61, "The bands of the wicked have robbed me: but I have not forgotten Thy law."** Wicked people treat the godly in many wicked ways. This is made plain in **2 Timothy 3:12-13: "Yea, and all that will live godly in Christ Jesus shall suffer persecution. 13 But evil men and seducers shall wax worse and worse, deceiving, and being deceived."** But behind the wickedness of the world of men there is a greater wickedness pulling the strings and manipulating events and the Bible exposes him in **Ephesians 6:10-12**:

> **Finally, my brethren, be strong in the Lord, and in the power of His might. 11 Put on the whole armour of God, that ye may be able to stand against the wiles of**

the devil. [12] **For we wrestle not against flesh and blood, but against principalities, against powers, against the rulers of the darkness of this world, against spiritual wickedness in high places.**

Whether the attempts to rob us come from visible wickedness, or the invisible activity of the demonic world, the response of the believer living in on-going revival is the same: **"I have not forgotten Thy law."** In the midst of the attacks and mistreatment that are part of living in this fallen world, surrounded by spiritual adversaries, I am to keep my heart and mind full of the Word of God. At the risk of redundancy, I'm going to quote again the verses from **2 Timothy 3** that I referenced on the previous page, but this time in their larger context:

> **Yea, and all that will live godly in Christ Jesus shall suffer persecution. [13] But evil men and seducers shall wax worse and worse, deceiving, and being deceived. [14] But continue thou in the things which thou hast learned and hast been assured of, knowing of whom thou hast learned them; [15] And that from a child thou hast known the holy scriptures, which are able to make thee wise unto salvation through faith which is in Christ Jesus. [16] All scripture is given by inspiration of God, and is profitable for doctrine, for reproof, for correction, for instruction in righteousness: [17] That the man of God may be perfect, throughly furnished unto all good works. (2 Timothy 3:12-17)**

Do you see the proper response to the persecution of the evil world around us? Just live in the pages of the inspired Word of God, because contained therein is everything needed to walk in victory and revival, no matter the circumstances.

Notice in our original text that the psalmist had confidence in the power of the Word of the Lord to enable him to keep on praising God through it all. **Verses 61-62** say it like this: **"The bands of the wicked have robbed me: but I have not forgotten Thy law. At midnight I will rise to give thanks unto Thee because of Thy righteous judgments."** Even **"at midnight,"** at the darkest of hours, when sleep eludes me and problems press in, I will find myself rising to praise my God and give Him thanks for His sovereign wisdom. It seems to me that rising **"at midnight"** to praise God represents more than the hour on the clock. Surely it stands for the proverbial "dark night of the soul," when things seem their worst and we are most tempted to lose heart and give in to despair. Even then, when things appear so bleak and confusing, if we will choose to stay focused on the Word of God, there is victory to be had and revival power to be experienced.

Many things happen to the children of God in the midnight hour. Jacob finally got his spiritual breakthrough after a late-night wrestling match with the angel of the Lord (**Genesis 32**), and Paul and Silas rocked a jailhouse with their midnight worship service (**Acts 16**). God help us not to wait until daybreak to praise Him and declare our trust in the fact that His judgments are righteous. No doubt there are many tears to be shed in the night as the attacks of the wicked fall upon us, but even in tears and heartache, we can give thanks by faith, if we forget not God's Word.

Having a heart for God, and walking in a lifestyle of revival, will cause me to worship and praise the Lord not only in the sunshine of ease and prosperity, but in the midnight of attack and suffering. My Lord, who is my portion, whose Word I hasten to obey, is always in absolute control of every aspect of my situation, including the attacks of my enemy. My worshipful confession is that His judgments are **"righteous"** — that His dealings with me are right, and that He never ceases to superintend my life and use all things for my good. And furthermore, my God will, with perfect righteousness, ultimately tend to all of the wicked who are attempting to harm me — and that includes the devil himself, and all who serve Satan's interests in the earth. Here is the end of the story:

> ...we ourselves glory in you in the churches of God for your patience and faith in all your persecutions and tribulations that ye endure: [5] Which is a manifest token of the righteous judgment of God, that ye may be counted worthy of the kingdom of God, for which ye also suffer: [6] Seeing it is a righteous thing with God to recompense tribulation to them that trouble you; [7] And to you who are troubled rest with us, when the Lord Jesus shall be revealed from heaven with His mighty angels, [8] In flaming fire taking vengeance on them that know not God, and that obey not the gospel of our Lord Jesus Christ: [9] Who shall be punished with everlasting destruction from the presence of the Lord, and from the glory of His power; [10] When He shall come to be glorified in His saints, and to be admired in all them that believe (because our testimony among you was believed) in that day. (2 Thessalonians 1:4-10)

Staying focused on the end of the journey will give power to any Christian to keep praising God through the midnight hour. Because one of these days "the midnight cry" is going to go out: **"Behold, the Bridegroom cometh; go ye out to meet Him."**[1] On that day, **Romans 8:17-18** will become more than words on a page:

> And if [we are] children, then heirs; heirs of God, and joint-heirs with Christ; if so be that we suffer with Him, that we may be also glorified together. [18] For I reckon that the sufferings of this present time are not worthy to be compared with the glory which shall be revealed in us.

---

[1] Matthew 25:6

4. My Peers.

These words of the psalmist in **verse 63** are precious to me: **"I am a companion of all them that fear Thee, and of them that keep Thy precepts."** The man of God said, "I'm choosing my peer group on purpose. I choose to identify myself with those who are serious about the Lord." Certainly the followers of Christ want to love all people, even those who set themselves to be our enemies. The New Testament records the plain teaching of Jesus on that point:

> **Ye have heard that it hath been said, Thou shalt love thy neighbour, and hate thine enemy. ⁴⁴ But I say unto you, Love your enemies, bless them that curse you, do good to them that hate you, and pray for them which despitefully use you, and persecute you; ⁴⁵ That ye may be the children of your Father which is in heaven: for He maketh His sun to rise on the evil and on the good, and sendeth rain on the just and on the unjust. ⁴⁶ For if ye love them which love you, what reward have ye? Do not even the publicans the same? ⁴⁷ And if ye salute your brethren only, what do ye more than others? Do not even the publicans so? ⁴⁸ Be ye therefore perfect, even as your Father which is in heaven is perfect. (Matthew 5: 43-48)**

We must be always willing to reach out in love and minister to any and all, even if we are cursed by them for our concern over their souls. These words of **Psalm 119:63** are not about refusing to speak or minister to someone who is unconverted or ungodly because of some high-minded idea that they are beneath us. To try to be a friend of sinners is to walk in the steps of the Savior, who **"came to seek and to save that which was lost"** **(Luke 19:10)**.

There is no place in Christianity for a holier-than-thou elitism that looks down on the unrighteous as unworthy of my love. But having said that, the psalmist made clear that when it came to companionship he would always be specific in his choice. To be **"a companion"** with someone is about more than casual acquaintance, passing conversation, or even intentional ministry. This is about where I go to find fellowship; this is the crowd with which I delight to keep company. I ought to love and serve anyone and everyone who will allow me, but I will **"companion"** only with those who give evidence that they genuinely fear the Lord and are seriously sold-out to glorifying Him in obedience.

> **Be ye not unequally yoked together with unbelievers: for what fellowship hath righteousness with unrighteousness? And what communion hath light with darkness? 15 And what concord hath Christ with Belial? or what part hath he that believeth with an infidel? 16 And what agreement hath the temple of God with idols? For ye are the temple of the living God; as God hath said, I will dwell in them, and walk in them; and I will be their God, and they shall be My people. 17 Wherefore come out from among them, and be ye separate, saith the Lord, and touch not the unclean thing; and I will receive you, 18 And will be a Father unto you, and ye shall be My sons and daughters, saith the Lord Almighty. (2 Corinthians 6:14-18)**

Those with a heart for God find themselves drawn to others who are like-minded. If I am living in spiritual awakening and walking in a lifestyle of revival, then one of the things that will mark my life is that I associate myself, in physical fellowship and spiritual kinship, with those who love the Lord Jesus with their all, and manifest that love in passionate, on-fire obedience to Him.

Notice that the psalmist confessed himself **"a compan-ion"** of **"all"** the God-fearing. Not just those who are rich and influential, but also those who are poor and despised by the world. Not only the well-known and sought after, but also those who will never be in the spot-light of public ministry. Not only those of his own skin color or ethnic group, but those from every background, race, and culture. They don't have to look just like me, come from my neighborhood or hemisphere, or even speak my language. All I need to know is that they love my Lord Jesus and long to live all-out for His glory.

Again, if you're living in revival you will always be burdened over souls, and will be found ministering to those who are openly rebellious against God, both without and within the church—but you can never find joyful fellowship with them. When it comes to companying with people, where your heart can be knit in unity and joyful communion, you must choose as your spiritual peer group those who are pressing on the upward way, whose lives reflect a passion to know the Lord intimately and please Him well. Your companions tell on you. The spiritual quality of the crowd with which you're comfortable and with whom you love to hang out reveals your own spiritual condition. **Proverbs 13:20** says, **"He that walketh with wise men shall be wise: but a companion of fools shall be destroyed."**

The concluding verse in this section of **Psalm 119** makes the glad-hearted confession that there is an overflowing plenty of God's mercy, and His Word is inexhaustible. **Verse 64** says, **"The earth, O LORD, is full of Thy mercy: teach me Thy statutes."** What a God we have to love and serve, how good and kind He is to His believing children, and how rich and helpful are the teachings of His Word! This is the real evidence of a soul living in on-going revival—a burning desire to keep on learning and growing; an insatiable hunger and thirst to be taught of the Lord.

For this cause we also, since the day we heard it, do not cease to pray for you, and to desire that ye might be filled with the knowledge of His will in all wisdom and spiritual understanding; [10] That ye might walk worthy of the Lord unto all pleasing, being fruitful in every good work, and increasing in the knowledge of God; [11] Strengthened with all might, according to His glorious power, unto all patience and longsuffering with joyfulness... (Colossians 1:9-11)

The cycle goes on and on—being filled with the knowledge of His will, responding in obedience to what is revealed, and then increasing in the knowledge of God.   Never ending, never running dry, always learning and growing—that's what revival is all about.   Our Redeemer is **"the fountain of living waters,"**[1] and to anyone who submits himself to Jesus in faith, He promised that **"out of his belly shall flow rivers of living water."**[2]

As always, the Word of God must be allowed to serve as a mirror which we use for personal reflection. So, these questions must be asked: Do you personally have a heart for God? Do you have an "amen!" to these verses in **Psalm 119**? Does this passage bear any resemblance to you? If so, glory to God for His work of mercy in your life; may you always keep following hard after Him. If not, cry out to Him for mercy, repent and turn your whole self over to Him in faith, call on Him for deliverance from the vanity of a wasted life, and surrender your all to Him at this very moment.   Let the example of Zacchaeus inspire you to do as that "wee little man" did when confronted with the call of Christ.

And when Jesus came to the place, He looked up, and saw him, and said unto him, Zacchaeus, make haste,

[1] Jeremiah 2:13

[2] John 7:38

and come down; for today I must abide at thy house. [6]And he made haste, and came down, and received Him joyfully. (Luke 19:5-6)

Chapter Nine

How to Faint-proof Your Heart

I began this book with a chapter drawn from a text that confronted the problem of perpetual backsliding. I'm going to end by drawing attention to a passage that reveals the key to perpetuating spiritual awakening. It is possible to actually live in revival, rather than just have occasional spasms of spiritual enthusiasm with long lulls of lukewarm religion in between. The question is how to prevent ourselves from fainting and falling out along the way. How can we keep from being overcome by the brutality of life in this sin-cursed world, and dragged down into discouragement and Christian mediocrity? There is help to be gleaned from **2 Corinthians 4:16-18**, which is the biblical text for this chapter:

> **For which cause we faint not; but though our outward man perish, yet the inward man is renewed day by day. [17] For our light affliction, which is but for a moment, worketh for us a far more exceeding and eternal weight of glory; [18] While we look not at the things which are seen, but at the things which are not seen: for the things which are seen are temporal; but the things which are not seen are eternal.**

The apostle spoke of refusing to **"faint,"** and gave particulars as to what caused them to not faint. The idea of "fainting" relates to revival the same way that night relates to day and cold to hot—they are mutually exclusive alternatives. To faint is to pass out, to lose consciousness and become insensitive and unresponsive to the immediate circumstances. To be revived is to regain consciousness, to wake up and be alert and active, to be vigorously alive. So, fainting is the enemy of revival, and living in revival means learning how to not faint.

The word **"faint"** in our text actually means "to become weary, lose heart, and give up in despair." A sister word to this one is found in **Galatians 6:9**: **"And let us not be weary in well doing: for in due season we shall reap, if we faint not."** The word for **"faint"** in **Galatians** means "to become weary with discouragement to the point of collapse." Obviously, to experience spiritual awakening (and live in revival) demands that the people of God face down the specter of fainting. The well-known verses of **Hebrews 12:1-3** speak of the revived Christian life in athletic terms:

> **Wherefore seeing we also are compassed about with so great a cloud of witnesses, let us lay aside every weight, and the sin which doth so easily beset us, and let us run with patience the race that is set before us, ²Looking unto Jesus the author and finisher of our faith; who for the joy that was set before Him endured the cross, despising the shame, and is set down at the right hand of the throne of God. ³For consider Him that endured such contradiction of sinners against Himself, lest ye be wearied and faint in your minds.**

Apparently, the prevention of faint-heartedness, and thus the maintaining of revival, is all about focus and perspective. When our eyes of faith are kept on Christ, and our perspective of life is heavenly and eternal, then we can stay free from the spiritual dropsy that would render us down for the count and out of the race.

The Apostle Paul shared three specific principles of Christian perspective that cause the born again to **"faint not."** I will speak of them in terms of mental focus.

1. Focus on the spiritual rather than the physical.

In **verse 16**, immediately following the announcement that fainting can be prevented, these words are found: **"though our outward man perish, yet the inward man is renewed day by day."** One thing is clear: if we would maintain revival and spiritual awakening, we must put greater emphasis on the inner man rather than the outer. That begs the question, what exactly is the outward man and inward man?

The **"outward man"** speaks of the physical self, the human body. This outer man is not the same thing as **"the old man"** spoken of in Scripture, and we mustn't confuse the two terms. The **"old man"** is the natural disposition toward sin and rebellion that all of us have inherited from our first father, Adam. **Ephesians 4:22-24** speaks of the necessity of putting off **"the old man, which is corrupt according to the deceitful lusts,"** and putting on **"the new man, which after God is created in righteousness and true holiness."** The old man is our proclivity to self-rule and spiritual stupidity, and it is seen as an opponent and alternative to the new man in Christ. In contrast, **"the outward man"** is set over against the **"the inward man."**

The outer man is not spoken of as inherently immoral, but it is decidedly mortal. This is simply a reference to the physical shell that encases the human soul and spirit; it is the part of us that can be literally seen and physically touched. Scripture uses **"the outward man"** to identify the intricate system of bones, organs, fluids, and tissues that make up my earthly body; the "me" that you can shake hands with, and that I take to the doctor for tests and treatment when I'm ill.

The **"inward man,"** then, is the spiritual self; the "real me" that animates my physical body and makes me who I am.

There's more to us than meets the eye. According to **Genesis 2:7**, **"the LORD God formed man of the dust of the ground, and breathed into his nostrils the breath of life; and man became a living soul."** The inner man speaks of this that God put into the physical shell that defines true life. In scriptural language, it is made up of soul and spirit. This **"inward man"** is invisible to the naked eye. No CT scan can measure its dimensions and no MRI can pin-point its exact location. But the moment the inner man vacates the outer man, everyone around knows that the real person is gone and all that is left is an empty carcass.

For the Christian, this term **"inward man"** is even more particular. It refers to the soul (the psychological self), but also to the spirit which is raised to life in Christ when a person gets born again. That's the point of **Ephesians 2:1-5**, which speaks of us as **"dead in trespasses and sins,"** until God in grace saved us and made us alive in Christ. **Colossians 3:1** describes true converts to Christ as those who are **"risen with"** Him, and in **John 5:24** the Lord Jesus Himself described the salvation of sinners in terms of passing **"from death unto life."** So, when the Bible speaks of the **"the inward man"** in the context of Christians, it is identifying not only the human psyche, but the human spirit that has been raised from the dead and quickened in Christ, indwelt with God's Holy Spirit, and empowered to perceive and interact with the kingdom of God.

With these scriptural concepts in mind, notice that Paul made a very realistic observation in the text at hand: the outer man is in the process of perishing. The word translated **"perish"** conveys the ideas of rotting, spoiling, and wasting away. Not very attractive, but that's life as we know it in this mortal flesh. The theological background for this reality is the curse of sin, which includes disease, decrepancy, and physical death. One day the victory of Jesus will be applied even to the visible bodies of those saved by grace, and all of the physical effects of sin will be forever banished. The wonderful promise is that one day this corruptible body will put on incorruption.[1] Even now, the Lord is merciful to heal many of our physical aches and illnesses; but even if God were to heal every disease of the body, still this outer man will eventually wear out and die.

Yet, just as it is inevitable for the outer man to waste away, it is possible and proper that the inner man should grow more and more robust and strong. **Ephesians 3:16** speaks of the possibility of believers being **"strengthened with might by His Spirit in the inner man."** John the Apostle wrote to a Christian brother who was obviously quite ill in the body, but doing well in the inner man: **"Beloved, I wish above all things that thou mayest prosper and be in health, even as thy soul prospereth."**[2] The text verse says, **"Yet the inward man is renewed day by day,"** and the word **"renewed"** has to do with restoration and empowerment, as in the promise of **Isaiah 40:28-31**:

> **Hast thou not known? Hast thou not heard, that the everlasting God, the LORD, the Creator of the ends of the earth, fainteth not, neither is weary? There is no searching of His understanding. [29] He giveth power to the faint; and to them that have no might He increaseth strength. [30] Even the youths shall faint and be weary, and the young men shall utterly fall: [31] But they that wait upon the LORD shall renew their strength; they shall mount up with wings as eagles; they shall run, and not be weary; and they shall walk, and not faint.**

As the years of mortal life go by, the outer man becomes increasingly aged and dilapidated, but the inner man of those who are born again becomes more youthful and vitally alive.

[1] 1 Corinthians 15:53

[2] 3 John 2

The principle of this passage, as it relates to not fainting and living in wide-awake revival, is that the key to it all is in putting emphasis and confidence in the spiritual rather than the physical. The simple fact is that, in order to overcome depression and discouragement, we've got to train ourselves to look beyond what is going on in our bodies and concentrate on what God is doing in our spirits. That is the real point of a couple of often misused New Testament passages:

> **Whose adorning let it not be that outward adorning of plaiting the hair, and of wearing of gold, or of putting on of apparel; 4 But let it be the hidden man of the heart, in that which is not corruptible, even the ornament of a meek and quiet spirit, which is in the sight of God of great price. (1 Peter 3:3-4)**

> **...exercise thyself rather unto godliness. 8 For bodily exercise profiteth little: but godliness is profitable unto all things, having promise of the life that now is, and of that which is to come. (1 Timothy 4:7b-8)**

There's nothing inherently evil about doing our best to be healthy and look presentable in public, unless that becomes our focus and obsession to the neglect of our spiritual condition. But who could deny that if most American Christians would spend even an equivalent amount of time and effort on our inner man as we do pouring time and resources into the outer man, we would have an outbreak of Holy Ghost revival within the week!

Victorious Christians, who live in a wide-awake, on-fire fellowship with Jesus, are those who learn to give their focused attention to spiritual things. As sure as you hold this book in your hand, your physical body is going to grow old and perish; and if your joy and hope is limited to how you look or feel in the body, then you're going to find that you are tempted to faint from discouragement sooner or later. But you have an inner man that does not age and need never become diseased and crippled. The way to perpetuate spiritual awakening over the long haul is to put priority on your internal relationship with the Lord, and willfully concentrate on allowing God's Spirit to fill and commune with your spirit. Revival requires that we each one learn to prioritize that part of us that will never be put in a casket and left in a graveyard.

2. Focus on the eternal rather than the temporary.

The middle verse in the trio that makes up our text says, **"For our light affliction, which is but for a moment, worketh for us a far more exceeding and eternal weight of glory."** Again, the Apostle Paul was very honest and realistic about Christian living in the here-and-now. He used the word **"affliction"** to speak of the common experience of all who live in this sin-cursed world, and that strong word is used variously to speak of suffering, trouble and tribulation. It is not uncommon to hear modern "faith" preachers say that believers ought to refuse to confess the reality of suffering and affliction; that we somehow create our problems with our confessions, and if we would only refuse to verbalize our trials they wouldn't be real. Of course, that is a very dangerous heresy that credits the creature with the ability to shape reality with the spoken word — which is something only the Creator can do. One thing is sure: Paul didn't hesitate to admit the reality of hardships and tribulation.

The interesting thing is the use of the adjective in this statement: **"our light affliction."** Those two words hardly belong together — **"light"** and **"affliction."** I don't know about you, but I have a hard time regarding any of my afflictions as **"light."** It's like speaking of "minor surgery" —

it's only minor if it's happening to you; if I'm having the surgery, there's nothing minor about it. If you didn't know anything about Paul's life and ministry, you might be tempted to think that he just had a charmed life and never had to deal with any serious problems. But if you have ever read of his career in the book of **Acts**, you know that Paul just seemed to go from the firing pan into the fire and back again. In a rare passage of self-revelation (**2 Corinthians 11:23-28**), Paul gave a brief synopsis of what life and ministry had held for him:

> **...in labors more abundant, in stripes above measure, in prisons more frequent, in deaths oft. 24 Of the Jews five times received I forty stripes save one. 25 Thrice was I beaten with rods, once was I stoned, thrice I suffered shipwreck, a night and a day I have been in the deep; 26 In journeyings often, in perils of waters, in perils of robbers, in perils by mine own countrymen, in perils by the heathen, in perils in the city, in perils in the wilderness, in perils in the sea, in perils among false brethren; 27 In weariness and painfulness, in watchings often, in hunger and thirst, in fastings often, in cold and nakedness. 28 Beside those things that are without, that which cometh upon me daily, the care of all the churches.**

And yet, in the context of all that, which by comparison makes my troubles pale almost into insignificance, Paul used the adjective **"light"** to speak of his sufferings.

The obvious key to Paul's victorious living is in perspective and priority focus. The Apostle wrote that these hardships were feather-weight and not too difficult to bear because he knew that they were **"but for a moment,"** and that they were contributing to **"a far more exceeding and eternal weight of glory."** In other words, Paul chose to focus his priority on eternity rather than the momentary.   The secret to long-term revival is defending against fainting, and learning how to not faint is dependent on training ourselves to think in terms of God's forever rather than being fixated on the right now.

None of us can really know the depth of heartache and sorrow that those around us have to bear. Each one of us has to deal with things that could crush us into the ground if it weren't for the sustaining grace of God. A wise man once said that we are all either in a personal storm, just coming out of a storm, or about to go into a storm. That's the nature of life on this planet. But regardless of the severity of the trial or the depth of the suffering, one word can be added to all of it — temporary! Heartache does not have the last word; affliction is not the final entry into your life journal; pain is not the period on the paragraph of any Christian's biography. The Apostle Paul, in the midst of constant heartache, hostility, and affliction, could walk on in radiant faith, living a lifestyle of spiritual awakening and Holy Ghost revival, because he had learned to take the long look.

Notice that Paul not only saw his affliction as brief in comparison to the eternity that waited just ahead, but furthermore he realized that his sufferings now were actually adding to his glory then. **"For our light affliction, which is but for a moment, worketh for us a far more exceeding and eternal weight of glory."** What a revelation! You mean that my hard times are not working _against_ me, but are working _for_ me?

> **The Spirit itself beareth witness with our spirit, that we are the children of God: [17] And if children, then heirs; heirs of God, and joint-heirs with Christ; if so be that we suffer with Him, that we may be also glorified together. [18] For I reckon that the sufferings of this present time are not worthy to be compared with the glory which shall be revealed in us. (Romans 8:16-18)**

Somehow, in the economy of God, every trial and hurt suffered faithfully now by His children will actually add to the **"glory"** that will be ours in eternity. That's why **Psalm 126:5** says, **"They that sow in tears shall reap in joy,"** and **Galatians 6:9** adds, **"In due season we shall reap, if we faint not."**

The enemies of the gospel, and those who are strangers to the faith-life, will mockingly say, "You're just talking about some 'pie-in-the-sky' fantasy that helps you ignore the real-life pain of the here-and-now." Others will look very pious and wise, and say, "Be careful. You can be so heavenly-minded that you're no earthly good." But the fact is that this life "from stem to stern" is but a moment, and there is an eternity to follow. The Lord Jesus taught us, **"Lay not up for yourselves treasures upon earth, where moth and rust doth corrupt, and where thieves break through and steal: But lay up for yourselves treasures in heaven, where neither moth nor rust doth corrupt, and where thieves do not break through nor steal: For where your treasure is, there will your heart be also."**[1] It's not being too heavenly-minded that sidelines the Christian and makes him no good on earth. The more we learn to put right here and now into the context of forever, then the more our earthly lives will be marked with the victory of Jesus and the anointing of the Spirit.

To be an overcomer who can honestly say, "I refuse to faint! I am determined to live in revival!" you must discipline yourself to look beyond the temporary hurts of life and focus on the eternal glory that God is preparing for you. Moses endured great hardship and stress, not only from the pagan world but from the people of Israel whom he was called to pastor, and the secret to his steadfastness is given in **Hebrews 11:24-26**:

---

[1] Matthew 6:19-21

> By faith Moses, when he was come to years, refused
> to be called the son of Pharaoh's daughter; 25Choosing
> rather to suffer affliction with the people of God, than
> to enjoy the pleasures of sin for a season; 26 Esteeming
> the reproach of Christ greater riches than the treasures
> in Egypt: for he had respect unto the recompence of
> the reward.

There's the key: Moses kept reminding himself that this life would soon be over, and there would then be **"the recompense of the reward"** awaiting in eternity.

Every Christian puts priority attention on one or the other — the right now, with its temporary suffering, or forever, where the glory of God's reward waits. To perpetuate spiritual awakening and live in revival, while in the middle of life's afflictions, necessitates an eternal outlook.

3. Focus on the invisible rather than the material.

The final verse in this text says, "**While we look not at the things which are seen, but at the things which are not seen: for the things which are seen are temporal; but the things which are not seen are eternal.**" The issue of eternality versus temporariness is the big deal, but along with that there is the matter of looking past what is visible to the natural eye in order to remind ourselves by faith of the greater significance of spiritual matters. It's paradoxical to speak of "looking" at something that can't be seen. Obviously the Apostle is not speaking of the function of his physical eyes, but of the focus of his faith. Recall that **Hebrews 11:1** defines **"faith"** as **"the evidence of things not seen,"** and later in the same chapter faith is given as the secret to Moses' spirituality, which was manifest in large part by the fact **"he endured as seeing Him who is invisible"** (Hebrews 11:27).

This is so foundational to Christianity that it is woven throughout the entire Word of God. There can be no pleasing God, no victorious living, no experience of revival, and no on-going spiritual awakening apart from living by faith. The one refrain that underscores all of the dealings of the Lord in the life of His redeemed is this key principle, recorded four times over in Scripture: **"the just shall live by his faith."**[1] The Christian life is a faith-life; it requires the divinely-given ability to see beyond the natural world to that which lies behind and back of physical creation. There must be a willingness to look past appearances to what is really true, because the invisible things of God are more real than that which can be seen, touched, tasted, smelled, and held in the hand. **2 Corinthians 5:7** puts it plainly: **"We walk by faith, not by sight."** Even though my physical feet must walk on many surfaces across the face of the earth, I must take every step "standing on the promises of God," reacting to every circumstance from the standpoint of utter confidence that what God has promised He will most certainly perform.

Living in a perpetual state of revival depends upon our commitment to focus on something beyond what our physical senses can register. If we become nothing more than sight-walkers, then inevitably we will replicate the terrible failure of Israel when it came time to cross over Jordan and inherit the Promised Land. An entire generation of Israel died under judgment because they let the testimony of their eyes overwhelm the testimony of the Lord, and they chose to believe what they could see over what God had said. A great contrast is drawn in **Philippians 3:17-21** between a group called **"the enemies of the cross of Christ"** and true disciples of Jesus, and part of it is expressed in these terms: the false religionists **"mind earthly things,"** but **"our conversation is in heaven, from whence also we look for the Savior."**

---

[1] Habakkuk 2:4, Romans 1:17, Galatians 3:11 and Hebrews 10:38.

Here is the third dividing line between believers who faint and those who maintain a wide-awake, revived spirituality. The ability to resist the gravitational pull of defeatism, which reduces the believer to dullness and spiritual mediocrity, is in large part predicated on the commitment to stay focused on the unseen—to walk by faith not by sight. The Apostle Paul could say, **"For which cause we faint not,"** because he had learned to keep his faith exercised by staying his heart and mind on the things of God rather than the things of this material world. One of the most precious of all God's great and precious promises is that of **Isaiah 26:3-4; "Thou wilt keep him in perfect peace, whose mind is stayed on Thee: because he trusteth in Thee. Trust ye in the LORD for ever: for in the LORD JEHOVAH is everlasting strength."** Walking by faith simply means keeping my mind **"stayed on"** the Lord, choosing to trust His promises and put all my confidence on the truth of His eternal Word. As soon as momentary, material things become the focal point of life, it chokes out the effectual working of the Word of God in my life.

> **And these are they which are sown among thorns; such as hear the word, [19] And the cares of this world, and the deceitfulness of riches, and the lusts of other things entering in, choke the word, and it becometh unfruitful. (Mark 4:18-19)**

For the Truth of God to bear fruit in my life, I must do some mental gardening; there are some briars that must be hoed up in order to make room for the working of the Word of the Lord. What that means is that I have to be willing to add my commitment to Paul's and say, **"We look not at the things which are seen, but at the things which are not seen."**